D0417874

Penguin Critica

The Poetry of Gerard Manley Hopkins

J. R. Watson is Professor of English, University of Durham. He is the author of various books on the Romantic period, including *Wordsworth's Vital Soul* (1982), and *English Poetry of the Romantic Period 1789–1830*. He is the editor of *Everyman's Book of Victorian Verse*, and he has made a tape on Hopkins' poetry for Norwich Tapes Ltd. His principal interests are in Romantic and Victorian poetry, especially with regard to landscape and hymnology.

Penguin Critical Studies

Advisory Editor:
Bryan Loughrey

Gerard Manley Hopkins

The Poetry of Gerard Manley Hopkins

J. R. Watson

Penguin Books

PENGUIN BOOKS

Published by the Penguin Group
Penguin Books Ltd, 27 Wrights Lane, London W8 5TZ, England
Penguin Books USA Inc., 375 Hudson Street, New York, New York 10014, USA
Penguin Books Australia Ltd, Ringwood, Victoria, Australia
Penguin Books Canada Ltd, 10 Alcorn Avenue, Toronto, Ontario, Canada M4V 3B2
Penguin Books (NZ) Ltd, 182–190 Wairau Road, Auckland 10, New Zealand

Penguin Books Ltd, Registered Offices: Harmondsworth, Middlesex, England

First published as a Penguin Masterstudy 1987
Reprinted as a Penguin Critical Study 1989
10 9 8 7 6 5 4 3 2

Copyright © J. R. Watson 1987
All rights reserved

Printed in England by Clays Ltd, St Ives plc
Filmset in Monophoto Times

Contents

Note to the Reader

All quotations from the poetry are taken from the Penguin edition of *Poems and Prose of Gerard Manley Hopkins*, edited by W. H. Gardner, first published in 1953. The other editions of Hopkins' work from which material has been taken are as follows:

The Letters of Gerard Manley Hopkins to Robert Bridges, edited by Claude Colleer Abbott, London, 1935 (abbreviated as L B)

The Correspondence of Gerard Manley Hopkins and Richard Watson Dixon, edited by Claude Colleer Abbott, London, 1935 (abbreviated as LD)

Further Letters of Gerard Manley Hopkins, edited by Claude Colleer Abbott, second edition, London, 1956 (abbreviated as F L)

The Journals and Papers of Gerard Manley Hopkins, edited by Humphry House and Graham Storey, London, 1959 (abbreviated as J P)

The Sermons and Devotional Writings of Gerard Manley Hopkins, edited by Christopher Devlin, S.J., London, 1959 (abbreviated as S D)

Introduction

The aim of this book is to give a short introduction to Hopkins' poetry. It begins with a brief chronicle of the events of his life, and attempts to draw conclusions, as far as this is possible, about the character of the man who wrote the poems. This is followed by a discussion of Hopkins' ideas: his religious beliefs, which underpin all his work, and his ideas on inscape and instress, sprung rhythm, poetic language and the sonnet form.

The third section of the book contains critical readings of individual poems. I have tried where possible to give indications about the meaning of a difficult passage, but I have not attempted anything like a 'reader's guide' or a full commentary on the poems (details of these will be found in the list of books at the end). In the first place, there is not sufficient room to permit this; and secondly, to paraphrase Hopkins is generally to lose the very thew and sinew of his verse. I have therefore chosen his major poems, and those which seemed to be most frequently read and discussed, and treated them individually with what I hope is useful comment: bearing in mind Pope's description of 'the better half of Criticism, namely the pointing out an Author's excellencies'.

J. R. Watson
Durham, 1 October 1985

1. Life, Character and Poetry

Gerard Manley Hopkins was born on 28 July 1844 at Stratford in south Essex. His father, Manley Hopkins, worked in an insurance office, and subsequently established his own firm. His mother, born Kate Smith, was the daughter of a doctor. Gerard was the eldest of eight children.

In 1852 the family moved from the flat plain east of London to the rolling hills and wooded heaths of Hampstead. Gerard was sent as a boarder to Highgate School nearby, where he stayed in the sixth form long enough to fall out with a dictatorial headmaster and to win a scholarship to Balliol College, Oxford. He went up to Oxford in April 1863, took a First in Honour Moderations (Greek and Latin) in December 1864 and a First in 'Greats' (Ancient History and Philosophy) in 1867. He seems to have made up his mind to become a Roman Catholic during the summer vacation of 1866, and was received into the Roman church on 21 October, following a brief and bitter correspondence with his shocked Anglican parents.

After leaving Oxford in 1867, he took up a post under his Roman Catholic mentor, John Henry Newman, as a teacher at the Oratory School, Birmingham; but he only survived the wear-and-tear of teaching for two terms. During the spring of 1868 he decided to apply to join the Jesuits, was accepted and entered the Order as a Novice on 7 September. After periods at Manresa House, Roehampton, and nearly three years at Stonyhurst in Lancashire, he went (in August 1874) to St Beuno's College in North Wales, looking over the beautiful vale of Clwyd. It was here that he began to write the poetry by which he is remembered: he had written a good deal in his early years, but destroyed it and resolved to write no more. This act of self-sacrifice and total dedication was brought to an end in December 1875 by a combination of unusual circumstances. The *Deutschland*, a German ship carrying five exiled nuns among its passengers, was wrecked on the Goodwin Sands at the mouth of the Thames, with the loss of many lives. Hopkins was much affected by the newspaper reports, and his Rector, Father Jones, happened to say that he wished someone would write a poem about it. The result was 'The Wreck of the Deutschland'. It was followed by a number of others during the next two years, before Hopkins' full ordination in September 1877.

After becoming a priest, Hopkins served in a number of parishes and other appointments at Sheffield, Stonyhurst, London, Oxford, Bedford Leigh (near Manchester) and Liverpool. At the end of this period, in August 1881, he began the 'Tertianship', a prolonged 'retreat' at Roehampton which lasted for a year. From 1882 to 1884 he taught at the College at Stonyhurst, and in 1884 he became Professor of Greek and Latin literature at University College, Dublin. This institution, founded by Newman to counter the influence of the Protestant Trinity College in Ireland, had been taken over by the Jesuits in 1883; Hopkins' tenure of the Chair was an arduous one, and he was probably weakened by worry and overwork when he fell ill at the end of April 1889. He died on 8 June.

What more is known about Hopkins' life and character is found partly in the recollections of a few friends, but principally in his own private and personal writings. These include his early notebooks, and his journal from 1866 to 1875; his sermons and religious writings; and his letters. The letters, principally those to Robert Bridges and to R. W. Dixon, provide by far the best commentary on Hopkins' poetry that has ever been written, and they will be frequently quoted in the chapters that follow. They also enable us to see more clearly Hopkins' unusual character and his marked individuality.

The first, and probably the most important, influence upon him was that of his parents and his family. Gerard was a first child, who perhaps never lost the sense of his own 'specialness', and whose relationship with his mother and father was intense and deeply affectionate. One result of this was that the great shaping event of his life, the conversion to Roman Catholicism, became a dividing event and a terrible crisis. His father's distraught letter of 18 October 1866, three days before the step was taken, ends 'O Gerard my darling boy are you indeed gone from me?' (FL 97) Its plangent tone indicates the degree of pain which his father was suffering, and is evidence of the corresponding depth of love that existed between them. Indeed, Gerard's own letter written on 16 October may have seemed so cold to his parents because he dared not give way to his deepest feelings for fear of changing his mind. He explains his position and tries to answer his parents' objections, but ends, 'I can still by no means make my pen write what I shd. wish.' (FL 95) C. C. Abbott, the editor of Hopkins' letters, described this one as 'written in ice' (FL xli), but the ice is only there to hold in the terrible heat of Hopkins' divided mind, sure of his direction in the faith but deeply conscious of the wounding of his parents' love. He told Newman that their letters to him were 'terrible: I cannot read them twice' (FL 29); and on the eve of his conversion he wrote to his mother:

12

Your letters, wh. shew the utmost fondness, suppose none on my part and the more you think me hard and cold and that I repel and throw you off the more I am helpless not to write as if it were true. In this way I have no relief. You might believe that I suffer too. (FL 100)

In due course, his parents came to accept the situation, and Gerard spent periods of leave at home, especially when recovering from illnesses; and in 1889 his parents were with him in Ireland when he died.

Second to the influence of his family was the powerful effect his education had upon him. As a boy at school, he had many friends. He was known by the nickname of 'Skin': 'one of the very best and nicest boys in the school,' a contemporary described him in after years, 'with his face always *set* to do what was right':

Tenacious when duty was concerned, he was full of fun, rippling over with jokes, and chaff, facile with pencil and pen, with rhyming jibe or cartoon; good, for his size, at games and taking his part, but not as we did placing them first. Quiet, gentle, always nice, and always doing his work well: I think he must have been a charming boy from a master's point of view, but he was completely changed by any wrong or ill treatment on their part. (FL 394-5)

The writer of this letter, C. N. Luxmoore, went on to demonstrate that the blustering and heavy-handed treatment of the boys by a bullying headmaster brought out the defiant and stubborn streak in Hopkins. He was always prepared to fight against injustice; and, like many schoolboys, he was often extreme in his reactions to authority. Subsequently, he reacted (as many people do) against the person that he had been at school: 'I had no great love for my schooldays and wished to banish the remembrance of them, even, I am ashamed to say, to the degree of neglecting some people who had been very kind to me.' (LD 12) This suggests the workings of a sensitive mind: his mature self wincing at the remembrance of his earlier years.

After the restrictions and rebellions of school, Oxford came as a relief and a liberation. As a Balliol man, Hopkins was a member of the most scholarly college in Oxford at the time, and he was taught by some very distinguished figures, including Benjamin Jowett, T. H. Green, and Walter Pater. It is possible that this increased his sense of his own distinctiveness: he admired excellence in others and sought it in himself, and his examination successes would have alerted him to the unusual nature of his own abilities. With this academic brilliance went a further consciousness of the privilege of living and studying in such a beautiful place. Oxford in the nineteenth century must have been delightful –

> *Towery city and branchy between towers;*
> *Cuckoo-echoing, bell-swarmèd, lark-charmèd, rook-racked, river-*
> *rounded;*

'Duns Scotus's Oxford'

– and generations of Oxford undergraduates celebrated its loveliness, ever afterwards associating it with their youthful and hopeful years. In Hopkins' case, the college gardens and the countryside around Oxford were an intense delight: he had already begun to show signs of talent as an artist, and the beauty of the natural world was eagerly captured in words and in drawings by his active and observant eye. His notebooks at that time have a most delicate sense of form and colour:

From Cumnor Hill saw St. Philip's and the other spires through blue haze rising pale in a pink light. On further side of the Witney road hills, just fleeced with grain or other green growth, by their dips and waves foreshortened here and there and so differenced in brightness and opacity the green on them, with delicate effect. On left, brow of the near hill glistening with very bright newly turned sods and a scarf of vivid green slanting away beyond the skyline, against which the clouds shewed the slightest tinge of rose or purple. Copses in grey-red or grey-yellow – the tinges immediately forerunning the opening of full leaf. (JP 133–4)

These pleasures were shared with like-minded friends, and Hopkins' letters at this time suggest a buoyant and boisterous humour, and a keen sense of fun; some of the friendships made at Oxford lasted throughout his life.

Alongside this happy undergraduate normality, a more serious side was always present, and developing fast. An entry in his journal for 6 November 1865 runs: 'On this day by God's grace I resolved to give up all beauty until I had His leave for it.' (JP 71) The suggestion of self-mortification here is confirmed by the strict discipline of his Lenten vows in the following January:

For Lent. No pudding on Sundays. No tea except if to keep me awake and then without sugar. Meat only once a day. No verses in Passion Week or on Fridays. No lunch or meat on Fridays. Not to sit in armchair except can work in no other way. Ash Wednesday and Good Friday bread and water. (JP 72)

His conversion to Roman Catholicism which followed a few years later was the natural result of immersing such an intense, fastidious and serious temperament in the troubled waters of Oxford religious life: in Oxford the different factions – Roman Catholic followers of Newman (who had been converted in 1845), Anglo-Catholics (led by E. B. Pusey), and the Broad Church and Evangelical movements – all contributed to the steamy atmosphere of controversy and debate. Beyond were the threats to religion from the scientific rationalism of Darwin and Huxley (*The Origin of Species* had been published in 1859); but the various parties of the church continued to tear one another apart with a decadent ferocity. Hopkins was deeply immersed in it all: in June 1864 he described Oxford as 'the head and fount of Catholicism in England and the heart of our Church' (FL 16–17). By 'our Church' he meant the Church of England, and especially the High Church or Anglo-Catholic part of it to which his family belonged.

This undergraduate religiosity led naturally to Hopkins' conversion to a church which claimed to be the one true church, tracing its authority back through the Apostolic Succession to St Peter himself and to the commands of Jesus Christ. He saw it (as converts sometimes do) as a matter of logic, but it was almost certainly a matter of temperament as well, of a need for religious and emotional certainty. The claims of the Roman Catholic church to truth and authority, and its disciplined codes of penitence, confession and absolution, would have appealed to Hopkins; his subsequent decision to join the Jesuits, with their severe code of obedience and dedication, was probably engendered by the same impulse that had made him fast in Lent. He needed to conquer himself, to subordinate his strong will (which had been shown in his behaviour at school) to the will of God and to the strenuous rule of the order. When he chose the Jesuits rather than the easier-going Benedictines, Newman wrote: 'Don't call "the Jesuit discipline hard", it will bring you to heaven. The Benedictines would not have suited you.' (FL 408)

'The Benedictines would not have suited you': the shrewd Newman had discerned in Hopkins' character that hankering after order, submission and discipline which was satisfied by joining the Jesuits. His intense and passionate selfhood was satisfied only by self-abnegation and surrender to the will of God; and his submission to the direction of the Order involved

such a sincere respect for authority as to accept its decisions and comply with them, not merely by outward performance but in all sincerity with the conviction that compliance is best, and that the command expresses for the time the will of God, as nearly as it can be ascertained. (JP 542)

So Hopkins felt that in surrendering himself to God and the Jesuit discipline he was actually fulfilling himself in a more profound way than if he had been following his normal human inclinations:

> *I seek no other liberty*
> *But that of being bound to Thee.*

These lines come from a hymn which is sometimes prefaced to the *Spiritual Exercises* of St Ignatius Loyola, the founder of the Jesuit Order. The *Spiritual Exercises* were, and are, the principal means of discipline and regeneration for a Jesuit; as their name implies, they are a spiritual training, the equivalent of exercise for an athlete or a soldier.

The rigorous and continued attention to the *Spiritual Exercises* can be seen to have been of fundamental importance to Hopkins' development as a poet, reinforcing the strong natural bent of his mind. Above all, they reminded the individual that he possessed three things:

an intellect capable of knowing, a heart formed for loving, a body endowed with wonderful senses.

Each of these receives its emphasis in the *Spiritual Exercises* and in Hopkins' poetry, where he is so acutely, almost exaggeratedly, aware of the mind, the heart and the senses. The *Exercises* require an effort of the imagination, the will and the heart; and in particular, they make demands of two kinds, the dramatic and the imaginative. The first prelude of the Fifth Exercise, for example, requires the devotee to present himself before God

like a criminal loaded with chains, brought from the dungeon of a prison and placed before the tribunal of his judge.

In just this way Hopkins begins his sonnet on *Jeremiah* 12:1, 'Thou art indeed just, Lord . . .'

> *Thou art indeed just, Lord, if I contend*
> *With thee; but, sir, so what I plead is just . . .*

But this is an unusual and isolated example. More widespread is the habit, in Ignatius and in Hopkins, of desiring to activate the imagination. Again and again, for example, the meditations on the life and Passion of Jesus Christ begin with words that are designed to bring a scene vividly before the mind: 'Represent to yourself'. The section on the birth of Jesus, for example, begins 'Represent to yourself the road from Nazareth to Bethlehem', and at a later stage in the meditation it continues:

Represent to yourself a ruinous stable, and at the end of it a manger, where Mary and Joseph are adoring the Son of God, who is lying in it between two animals.

The 'Application of the Senses on the Birth of Jesus Christ' then goes on to apply to this scene a detailed examination by sight, hearing, taste and touch. Hopkins' sermons often do this: 'And now, brethren,' he writes of the feeding of the five thousand, 'think you see them like a well drilled army encamped on the green field . . .' (SD 231)

The *Spiritual Exercises*, therefore, had a profound effect upon Hopkins, upon his imagination and upon his way of experiencing the world. The Jesuit discipline also encouraged a certain extremism in his character, which was evidenced in his need for total commitment. It was this which led Hopkins to destroy his early poems. A cryptic note in his journal at the time he was deciding to be a religious and a Jesuit in particular (11 May 1868) refers to the 'Slaughter of the innocents' (JP 165), which suggests that he was destroying his poems, killing off the innocent children of his imagination. 'I saw they wd. interfere with my state and vocation,' he told Bridges in the same year (LB 24). It was all part of a complete dedication; not only had he destroyed his poems in 1868, but he had decided to give up poetry for the future, a sacrifice of his dearest art to God:

What I had written I burnt before I became a Jesuit and resolved to write no more, as not belonging to my profession, unless it were by the wish of my superiors; . . . (LD 14)

Fortunately it *was* the wish of his superior on one accidental occasion, and 'The Wreck of the Deutschland' was the result. But the refusal of the Roman Catholic periodical *The Month* to publish it must have been something of a blow to a poet who took such pride in his work; this failure to publish may have increased Hopkins' uneasiness at the conjunction within himself of two contrary impulses, his creativity (which involved an appreciation of beauty, craftsmanship, form, and was a thing he loved and enjoyed doing) and the self-sacrifice of the Jesuits.

The adolescent resolution to give up all beauty until he had God's leave for it was an early indication of this urge to sacrifice his earthly loves to the higher demands of a spiritual discipline. At some time, however, Hopkins must have become convinced that the beauty of the created world could be enjoyed without betraying his religion, indeed that it could be enjoyed as evidence of the presence of God in created things. The journals are full of examples, of which the following is probably the most celebrated:

I do not think I have ever seen anything more beautiful than the bluebell I have been looking at. I know the beauty of our Lord by it. Its inscape is mixed of strength and grace, like an ash tree. The head is strongly drawn over backwards and arched down like a cutwater drawing itself back from the line of the keel. The lines of the bells strike and overlie this, rayed but not symmetrically, some lie parallel. They look steely against the paper, the shades lying between the bells and behind the cocked petal-ends and nursing up the precision of their distinctness, the petal-ends themselves being delicately lit. Then there is the straightness of the trumpets in the bells softened by the slight entasis and by the square play of the mouth. (JP 199)

This kind of perception – delicate, detailed, loving – can be seen not only in Hopkins' poems but also in his drawings and paintings, which are often small and exquisite in their observation and execution; for in such an attentive observation the poet found the beauty he was seeking. He was strongly influenced in this by the ideas and practices of Ruskin, who advocated a detailed study of nature and a truthful representation of it, and who produced his own drawings and paintings in support of his principles. And in Hopkins' poetry, the work of the eye is extremely important: its sense of colour and contrast, and of particular and minute appearances, is a reminder of the importance to him of the sight, 'of áll my eyes see' ('Ash-boughs', line 1).

In addition to drawing and painting, Hopkins was also a musician, who played the piano and at one time began to learn the violin. He composed a number of settings to poems by Bridges, Dixon, and himself, and towards the end of his life music took up a good deal of his creative time. The importance of this is that Hopkins had a musician's ear as well as a painter's eye: his poetry was written not only to celebrate appearances, but also to demonstrate, with feeling and precision, the movement or sound of things, the melody and rhythm of a poetic line, and the placing of a line within the pattern of sound in a verse. He insisted continually that his poetry was to be read aloud, or recited, and not perused silently; sometimes he suggested a musical time for it, such as *tempo rubato* (flexible time) or *adagio molto*.

His attention to beauty in natural objects, and his love of poetry, painting, and music, meant that Hopkins was extraordinarily sensitive to the destruction of lovely things or the neglect of them. This may be seen in many of his poems, where the impress of man upon the simplicity of nature means that

> *. . . all is seared with trade; bleared, smeared with toil;*
>> 'God's Grandeur'

and this is most notably seen in 'Binsey Poplars', where the cutting-down of a row of beautiful trees is wounding and painful, and the result is that

> *After-comers cannot guess the beauty been.*

Hopkins was not only wounded by such things; he was a fastidious man, picking his way through life with his cassock slightly lifted. In a letter to Bridges he remembered some of the squalid city streets of the industrial north:

as I went up Brunswick Road (or any street) at Liverpool on a frosty morning it used to disgust me to see the pavement regularly starred with the spit of the workmen going to their work; and they do not turn aside, but spit straight before them as you approach, as a Frenchman remarked to me with abhorrence and I cd. only blush. . . . And our whole civilisation is dirty, yea filthy, and especially in the north; for is it not dirty, yea filthy, to pollute the air as Blackburn and Widnes and St. Helen's are polluted and the water as the Thames and the Clyde and the Irwell are polluted? (LB 299)

This last point is a political one. Hopkins was a contradiction in politics, as in so many other things: he believed in radical reform, and described himself as 'in a manner . . . a Communist'. But he prefaced this by 'Horrible to say': 'Horrible to say, in a manner I am a Communist.' (LB 27) He could see very clearly the injustices of a system in which the poor were not allowed to benefit from the wealth which they created, but he disliked politicians and shrank from the violence that went with revolution. In a letter to Bridges he spoke of 'Loafers, Tramps, Cornerboys, Roughs, Socialists and other pests of society' (LB 274).

The picture which emerges from a study of Hopkins' life and character is therefore a complex one: a first child, conscious of his own special selfhood and distinctiveness, a great lover of beauty, talented as an artist and musician as well as a poet, profoundly influenced by the religious temper of his own time and attempting to lose himself in the discipline of the most severe religious order. The *Spiritual Exercises* of St Ignatius encouraged his creative imagination: yet his own sense of duty seems to have made him uneasy at the dual vocation of priest and poet. 'There is evidence,' wrote C. C. Abbott, 'of a determined effort to coerce his poetry into narrowly Roman Catholic channels, as if here might be found appeasement and equilibrium for both sides of his nature.' (LB xxxi) Yet it would be too simple to say that Hopkins the Jesuit spoiled Hopkins the poet: in many ways his deepest responses to nature were awakened, not just by a contemplation of the event or the object, but by a *religious* contemplation of that event or object.

Hopkins' poetry can be seen to be related to certain features of his character. In particular we may observe his passionate desire for truth: Hopkins will have no truck with half-truths or imprecise utterance, with

19

emotions half-expressed or with vague descriptions. His poetry has to be as exact as possible, piercingly and often disquietingly truthful about the world and about himself. He looks for a word or image which will record something with precision, so that it can be immediately recognized or be seen as if for the first time, such as 'rose-moles all in stipple upon trout that swim', or the 'windpuff-bonnet of fawn-froth' as the burn tumbles down at Inversnaid. Hopkins was a great nature poet and a great landscape poet: that is, he succeeds in depicting the natural scene, with its movement, its atmosphere and its character, and he succeeds too in conveying a sense of local landscape, with great sensitivity and feeling. The names of his poems are a testimony to this: they record particular places, Inversnaid, Ribblesdale, Binsey (*Landscape and Inscape*, by Milward and Schoder, has photographs of these places; see Suggestions for Further Reading).

But Hopkins does not only see nature: he has an acute eye for people (Felix Randal, Harry Ploughman) and for what they do (Hopkins was very much aware of work as a shaping force in a person's life). Even more important, perhaps, was his expertise in self-examination (encouraged, of course, by his Jesuit discipline and the *Spiritual Exercises*) which gave him an uncanny watchfulness over his own moods and feelings. He dexterously finds words to express (often with the most powerful physical images) the sense of joy, happiness, frustration, misery or relief. In all these moods, Hopkins was attempting to register the truth as he saw and felt it, as exactly and precisely as possible, the expression of his nerve endings.

These are, of course, *his* nerve endings especially, *his* perception, his own very strong individual specialness; and the language is his too. Ordinary language is often imprecise, and therefore lifeless: Hopkins was attempting to restore some accuracy to it by using the words he chooses in the way that he does. Here again he was often aware of being different, and he knew that he was open to the charge of being odd in his poetic diction. But he was a determined and stubborn person, as well as a gentle and sensitive one: and in many of his ideas and expressions he refused to be budged from what he thought was right. He defended his poetry stoutly against Bridges' criticism, and often rightly: but it is difficult to avoid the feeling at times that Hopkins really would *not* listen, so that his poetry is sometimes over-compressed and sometimes obscure. We can deduce something of this from the letters of Sir Robert Stewart, who had looked at Hopkins' music, made some criticisms of it and been duly rebuked. Stewart wrote back, pleasantly and sharply:

I saw, ere we had conversed ten minutes on our first meeting, that you are one of those special pleaders who never believe yourself wrong in any respect. You always excuse yourself for anything I object to in your writing or music so I think it a pity to disturb you in your happy dreams of perfectability   nearly everything in your music was wrong   but you will not admit that to be the case – (FL 427)

In his poetry Hopkins was usually right: gloriously right on some occasions, and far more frequently than Bridges would give him credit for. At times, however, he was wrong, and there are some parts of his poetry which are more difficult or obscure than they should be, and others which are more strongly expressed than they need be, especially the anti-Protestant ones.

On the whole, however, Hopkins knew he was right (and generally was right) because he was writing a poetry which involved his mind, his body and his soul. He brought to his poetry a really fine mind, trained at Oxford in Latin, Greek and ancient philosophy, and sharpened in subsequent years on the grindstone of Jesuit theology; he brought to it a body, sensitive to all weathers and equipped with finely-tuned senses of hearing, touch, taste and sight; and he brought to it a heart full of enthusiasm, loving beauty, but open also to misery and depression. Above all, perhaps, he brought a strong sense of himself:

I find myself both as man and as myself something most determined and distinctive, at pitch, more distinctive and higher pitched than anything else I see; . . . (SD 122)

This is where he started from: from the inescapable self-hood, with all its wonderful 'selving':

And this is much more true when we consider the mind; when I consider my self being, my consciousness and feeling of myself, that taste of myself, of *I* and *me* above and in all things, which is more distinctive than the taste of ale or alum, more distinctive than the smell of walnutleaf or camphor, and is incommunicable by any means to another man (as when I was a child I used to ask myself: What must it be to be someone else?). Nothing else in nature comes near this unspeakable stress of pitch, distinctiveness and selving, this self being of my own. (SD 123)

The dark side of this unavoidable identity is, of course, the sensitivity which causes unhappiness and despair: and the 'terrible sonnets' witness the way in which Hopkins suffered periods of anguish and grief when his self-hood became almost insupportable. But both in praise and in anguish, Hopkins was conscious of the power and energy of God, in His creation of the varied world or in His wrestling with the stubborn soul. And since Hopkins' poetry was written, principally, to the glory of God, and in praise and reverence of Him, the next section will consider his religious ideas in more detail; this will be followed by a section on his poetic and technical ideas.

2. Hopkins' Religious Beliefs

Hopkins' most intimate and revealing spiritual dilemmas and problems will never be known, for his confessional notebooks were burnt (as he instructed) after his death. What can be gathered from his letters suggests that the Jesuit life was for him the best way of life (as Newman had seen), and its training and discipline is found everywhere in his poetry, not only in the underlying modes of perception (strengthened by the *Spiritual Exercises*) but in the actual doctrinal positions which underpin the poetry. I have therefore chosen to examine Hopkins' religious beliefs under the orthodox headings of God the Father, God the Son, and God the Holy Spirit.

God the Father

For Hopkins, God is almighty, wonderful and incomprehensible. He is the 'past all/Grasp God' ('Wreck', stanza 32), the figure who is behind and beyond all things, whose nature we can only dimly understand. The Trinity itself is a mystery, God the 'three-numberèd form' ('Wreck', stanza 9).

Human beings know God in two ways. In the first place they know Him as their master and Lord: He is the other force which is felt in the struggles of the self, as the poet lies 'wrestling with (my God!) my God'. The figure comes from the Biblical account of wrestling Jacob (Genesis 32:24–30), and indicates how in the spirit, human beings can come close to God (as wrestlers to each other) in struggling with Him. Hopkins' conception of God is therefore one of a force which is placed over against him: just as he felt the power and 'pitch' of his own selfhood strongly, so he feels the power and pitch of the 'other', God, as master and king.

The duty of man, and of the world, is 'reverence, praise and service':

the world, man, should after its own manner give God being in return for the being he has given it or should give him back that being he has given. This is done by the great sacrifice. (SD 129)

The great sacrifice is the surrender of the self to the will of God, even as Jesus Christ, although he was God

22

emptied or exhausted himself so far as that was possible, of godhead and behaved only as God's slave, as his creature, as man, which also he was, and then being in the guise of man humbled himself to death, the death of the cross. It is this holding of himself back, and not snatching at the truest and highest good, the good that was his right, nay his possession from a past eternity in his other nature, his own being and self, which seems to me the root of all his holiness and the imitation of this the root of all moral good in other men. (SD 108)

The inspiration of this passage is St Paul's great commentary on the Incarnation in Philippians 2:5-11. It requires from the poet a profound and all-consuming devotion, a sacrifice which surrenders all self-will in accepting God in both terror and love. God is Master and Lord in 'The Wreck of the Deutschland' (following St John 13:13: 'Ye call me Master and Lord: and ye say well; for so I am'); He is Lord of life and death ('Wreck', stanza 1). He can strike men down, as He struck St Paul

> *with an anvil-ding . . .*
> *as once at a crash Paul,*
> 'Wreck', stanza 10

and He can pursue man, so that his heart is 'hard at bay' ('Wreck', stanza 7) as if hunted.

God is present in the human soul, yet He is also beyond and above all its imaginings:

a being so intimately present as God is to other things would be identified with them were it not for God's infinity or were it not for God's infinity he could not be so intimately present to things. (SD 128)

God, we might say (over-simplifying but attempting to see this more clearly) is present because the human soul recognizes that which is greater than itself within itself: it is God's infinite power that allows Him to be 'present to things' yet He cannot be specifically identified with them because He is God, above and beyond all things.

The second way of knowing God, therefore, is in His creatures and His created world. 'All things were made by him; and without him was not any thing made that was made.' (St John 1:3) He commmands the elements: it is His thunder ('Wreck', stanza 5) and His storm and cold ('Wreck', stanza 17): the duty of man is to struggle to understand this magnificence and mystery:

> *Since, tho' he is under the world's splendour and wonder,*
> *His mystery must be instressed, stressed;*
> *For I greet him the days I meet him, and bless when I understand.*

Many of Hopkins' finest and best-known poems are recordings of moments when he meets God and greets Him; and in the journals, letters and notebooks there are moving and memorable references to God in creation:

As we drove home the stars came out thick: I leant back to look at them and my heart opening more than usual praised our Lord to and in whom all that beauty comes home. (JP 254)

God is therefore 'beauty's self and beauty's giver' ('The Leaden Echo and the Golden Echo'): He is everywhere, in the ground we walk upon and the air we breathe. All the lovely dappled, alternating, changing and shifting things in the world come from God:

> *Whatever is fickle, freckled (who knows how?)*
> *With swift, slow; sweet, sour; adazzle, dim;*
> *He fathers-forth whose beauty is past change:*
> *Praise him.*

God is eternal and timeless, yet He exists within our time, because He is of our world as well as beyond it. Hopkins' beautiful image for this is that of a river flowing through a lake:

Time has three dimensions and one positive pitch or direction. It is therefore not so much like any river or any sea as like the Sea of Galilee, which has the Jordan running through it and giving a current to the whole. (SD 196)

The three dimensions are presumably past, present and future, and the pitch or direction is God's purpose, which runs through it. And as a river keeps the lake clean and unpolluted, so God operates through time; yet to see them as a river would be to see Him as linear:

But rather as the light falls from heaven upon the Sea of Galilee not only from the north, from which quarter the Jordan comes, but from everywhere, so God from every point, so to say, of his being creates all things. (SD 196)

So the power and mystery of God is felt as His *stress*, which 'rides time like riding a river' ('Wreck', stanza 6). The response to this is a response not from the mind but from the heart; response from the mind is impossible, because God is beyond all knowing, mysterious and holy, but the heart responds in a way which the poet recognizes as utterly authentic:

> *My heart in hiding*
> *stirred for a bird, – the achieve of, the mastery of the thing!*
> 'The Windhover', lines 7–8

In 'The Wreck of the Deutschland' it is the heart which, hard at bay (pursued by God), is 'out with it' (stanza 8), that is filled to bursting with the power of God in redemption, 'The dense and the driven Passion, and frightful sweat' (stanza 7). The heart is 'mother of being in me' (stanza 18), that is the origin of all his *being*, his real existence in God, his feeling life. It is the heart that suffers in the terrible sonnets: it is the heart which feels the power of God and the stubbornness of human selfishness.

The problem of human sin and selfishness is one that Hopkins felt acutely. To him it was particularly noticeable in the blindness of mankind to beauty, in the dreary drudgery of some lives, and in the way in which lovely things were destroyed. In 'Ribblesdale', for instance, the beautiful Lancashire valley is depicted as longing for the coming of God; but mankind is

> *To his own self bent so bound, so tied to his turn,*
> *To thriftless reave both our rich round world bare*
> *And none reck of world after, . . .*

Man is so selfish that he plunders ('reaves') the present world until it is bare, and he cares nothing for the hereafter, heaven or hell. Similarly he destroys a grove of poplars beside the river, so that

> *After-comers cannot guess the beauty been.*
> 'Binsey Poplars'

Clearly, one of Hopkins' intentions in writing his poetry was to reawaken his readers' attention to beauty, and this became in itself a religious action, worthy of a priest.

More serious than the customary neglect of beauty, however, was the inner resistance of human beings to God. Since we live in a fallen world, we are all inclined to sin, and Hopkins, as a Jesuit priest accustomed to self-examination, was acutely aware of his own shortcomings. The truth is uncompromising: 'if you are in sin you are God's enemy, you cannot love or praise him' (SD 240). You are in danger of being not fully human, because the full humanity of man is found in doing the will of God, whereas 'the wicked and the lost are like halfcreations and have but a half being' (SD 197).

God the Son

The natural tendency of mankind to sin is countered by God's grace in coming to earth in the person of Jesus Christ. Christ is 'the first intention

25

of God outside himself, or, as they say, *ad extra*, outwards, the first outstress of God's power' (SD 197). Yet his life on earth involved 'mystery and humiliation':

Christ then like a good shepherd led the way; but when Satan saw the mystery and the humiliation proposed he turned back and rebelled ... (SD 197)

Christ is not only a shepherd, but a hero:

> *Pride, rose, prince, hero of us, high-priest,*
> *Our hearts' charity's hearth's fire, our thoughts' chivalry's throng's Lord.*
> 'Wreck', stanza 35

His presence can be found everywhere, in beauty and in suffering: the main point of 'The Wreck of the Deutschland' is that Christ comes to the tall nun, and to the others as well

> *Our passion-plungèd giant risen,*
> *The Christ of the Father compassionate, fetched in the storm of his strides.*
> 'Wreck', stanza 33

He can produce terror in man ('Wreck', stanza 2), but through that terror comes a greater sense of the presence of God, of Christ himself: his *mastery* and his *mercy* are allied, just as the sounds of the words are similar. He brings light in darkness, warmth in winter ('Wreck', stanza 9), and above all, he has an interest in the welfare of mankind: even when he is disregarded, he follows them

> *éyes them, heart wánts, care haúnts, foot fóllows kínd,*
> *Their ránsom, théir rescue, ánd first, fást, last friénd.*
> 'The Lantern out of Doors'

The aim of all God's actions through Christ is the freeing of the self to be true to its deepest and noblest instincts:

For grace is any action, activity, on God's part by which, in creating or after creating, he carries the creature to or towards the end of its being, which is its selfsacrifice to God and its salvation ... It is as if a man said: That is Christ playing at me and me playing at Christ, only that is no play but truth; That is Christ *being me* and me being Christ. (SD 154)

Such grace works in three ways: quickening, 'and stimulating towards good'; corrective, 'turning the will from one direction or putting into another'; and elevating, 'which lifts the receiver from one cleave of being to another and to a vital act in Christ':

this is truly God's finger touching the very vein of personality, which nothing else can reach . . . (SD 158)

Hopkins touches the finger of God in the first stanza of 'The Wreck of the Deutschland': this is part of the process of continual discovery and rediscovery of God's grace. In 'The Blessed Virgin Compared to the Air we Breathe', he describes how

> . . . we are wound
> With mercy round and round
> As if with air: . . .

and the Incarnation, in which Jesus Christ was born of a pure virgin, is a process, like breathing, which goes on and on, inseparable from life itself:

> Of her flesh he took flesh:
> He does take fresh and fresh,
> Though much the mystery how,
> Not flesh but spirit now
> And makes, O marvellous!
> New Nazareths in us,
> Where she shall yet conceive
> Him, morning, noon, and eve;
> New Bethlems, and he born
> There, evening, noon, and morn –
> Bethlem or Nazareth,
> Men here may draw like breath
> More Christ and baffle death; . . .

Hopkins' imagination delights in the paradoxical idea that Christ can be born in us again and again, at every moment: the idea is impossible in any physical sense, but its spiritual meaning is clear. Hopkins' especial quest is to find an image which will express this spiritual truth, as he does in his Commentary on 'Contemplation for Obtaining Love' from the *Spiritual Exercises*:

Suppose God shewed us in a vision the whole world inclosed first in a drop of water, allowing everything to be seen in its native colours; then the same in a drop of Christ's blood, by which everything whatever was turned scarlet, keeping nevertheless mounted in the scarlet its own colour too. (SD 194)

In all his accounts of the Incarnation, Hopkins naturally responds to the symbolic nature of biblical and Christian language, so that here the drop of Christ's blood becomes a world in itself, *the* world itself (for the drop of Christ's blood contains the world within itself), somehow dipped in blood yet also itself. This is an imaginative extension of the idea of sinners (or the sinful world) being washed in the blood of the sacrificial Lamb (as in Revelation 7:14) in which *blood* washes *white*:

These are they which came out of great tribulation, and have washed their robes, and made them white in the blood of the Lamb.

Of all the symbols for Christ, the most important in Hopkins' writing is that of Christ as king. In the commentary on 'The Kingdom of Christ' in the *Spiritual Exercises*, he suggests that the mind should concentrate on an ideal human king, and then apply the same response to Christ: the awareness of the king, of his greatness and his nobility, is fundamental to Hopkins' poetry. It is the crowning glory of 'The Wreck of the Deutschland' that the tall nun, and through her the poet, is vouchsafed a glimpse of such royalty:

> *look at it loom there,*
> *Thing that she . . . there then! the Master,*
> Ipse, *the only one, Christ, King, Head:*
> > 'Wreck', stanza 28

This is the sight of the reality that comes from the suffering and the shipwreck: and Christ in majesty, his authority and nobility, is forever present to Hopkins' mind.

To respond to such majesty is a subject's duty, yet it also involves something greater than mere obedience, a full-hearted loyalty and love which comes from within. This is the operation of the Holy Spirit.

God the Holy Spirit

If God is the master of all things, the great unknowable, past man's thought, and Christ is the king, then the Holy Spirit is a presence and a fire. In 'God's Grandeur', the poet observes that the world is full of God's grandeur but that it is unnoticed; however, nature is always a sign of the presence of God, and light can come out of darkness as morning succeeds night.

> *Because the Holy Ghost over the bent*
> *World broods with warm breast and with ah! bright wings.*

The Holy Ghost is active, inspiring, like Christ himself, in fact a part of the divinity. Hopkins uses a delightful and homely image from cricket to describe it, the Holy Ghost as Paraclete or Comforter:

you have seen at cricket how when one of the batsmen at the wicket has made a hit and wants to score a run, the other doubts, hangs back, or is ready to run in again, how eagerly the first will cry Come on, come on! – a Paraclete is just that, something that cheers the spirit of man, with signals and with cries, all zealous that he should do something and full of assurance that if he will he can, calling him on, springing to meet him half way, crying to his ears or to his heart: This way to do God's will, this way to save your soul, come on, come on! (SD 70)

In the same way, says Hopkins, Jesus 'cried men on' (SD 70); his cry is not only to the ears but to the heart. The traditional image of the heart warmed, and the heart on fire, is stirred to new life by Hopkins. 'The Wreck of the Deutschland' ends with the description of Christ the king as

> *Our hearts' charity's hearth's fire, . . .*
> stanza 35

And in 'The Windhover', the bird soars or swoops

> *. . . AND the fire that breaks from thee then, a billion*
> *Times told lovelier, more dangerous. O my chevalier!*

His sermon on the Holy Ghost, dated 25 April (1880) takes a text from St John 16:8, referring to the Comforter (the Holy Spirit, the Paraclete): 'And when he is come, he will reprove the world of sin, and of righteousness, and of judgment.' Hopkins' exposition of this text is simple, yet effective. The Holy Ghost comes, he says, to do good in the face of sin; to encourage goodness and justice; and to have in mind God's judgment as a bait and a spur: 'There is the bait or prize of hope, the crown in heaven for the just, and there is the spur of fear, the fire of hell for the sinner.' (SD 71–2) And to accomplish this, the Holy Ghost continues to operate in the world: to bring about the task of convincing the world of sin, of justice and of judgment. This task was begun by God the Son in his life, but is now carried on by the same almighty power, for the Father, the Son and the Holy Ghost 'are not three almighties, but one almighty' (SD 72).

This interpretation of the spirit and working of the Holy Ghost accords, as might be expected, with the beliefs in Hopkins' poetry. He sees spring, for example, as a season of new life, a sinless moment of joy like the garden of Eden before the Fall; and he thinks by analogy of children, in the springtime of their lives:

> *. . . Have, get, before it cloy,*
> *Before it cloud, Christ, lord, and sour with sinning,*
> *Innocent mind and Mayday in girl and boy,*
> *Most, O maid's child, thy choice and worthy the winning.*
>
> 'Spring'

In addition to this powerful awareness of innocence, and conversely of sin, Hopkins has an equally strong sense of justice or righteousness. God's judgment is felt by all, in Hopkins' view. It is a precondition of life, a force in life which gives it meaning and purpose. It requires an assent to good and a renunciation of evil, the *yes* or *no* of 'The Wreck of the Deutschland':

> *. . . Oh,*
> *We lash with the best or worst*
> *Word last!*
>
> 'Wreck', stanza 8

So too, in 'The Loss of the Eurydice', the poet notes that a 'duty-swerver' can change and act heroically:

> *It is even seen, time's something server,*
> *In mankind's medley a duty-swerver,*
> *At downright 'No or yes?'*
> *Doffs all, drives full for righteousness.*

The triple operation of the Holy Ghost is not always explicit, but it is present everywhere in Hopkins' thinking. It is, for him, a mysterious and holy power (by mysterious he means holy, unfathomable, incomprehensible) and his text is a 'mysterious text': and because of its very nature, his sermon is capable of an almost infinite extension. He is forced to conclude at the usual end-of-sermon time:

I should shew too the manner of his convincing the world, the thousand thousand tongues he speaks by and his countless ways of working, drawing much more than I have drawn from my mysterious text, but I must forbear: yet by silence or by speech to him be glory who with the Father and the Son lives and reigns for ever and ever. Amen. (SD 75)

This sentence may serve as an emblem for much of Hopkins' life and work: his poetry and his other writings suggest that his ideas of God in Creation, Christ in Redemption and the Holy Ghost in continuous working are capable of endless exposition and exploration: we must be thankful that so much formed expression in speech rather than silence.

3. Techniques and Poetic Language

We have seen that certain formative influences upon Hopkins led to a particular kind of poetry: extremely individual, written by an imagination that was encouraged by the *Spiritual Exercises* to develop its reconstructive power, and remarkably observant. The conscious application of the powers of observation and recording is found in the poetry, but also in the important ideas of 'inscape' and 'instress'. Together with 'sprung rhythm', and the peculiar use of language, these features provide the reader with a set of tools to get at the complex mechanism of Hopkins' poetry.

Inscape and instress

The first example of the use of the words 'inscape' and 'instress' in Hopkins' writings comes in his notes, dated 1868, on the Greek philosopher Parmenides:

His great text, which he repeats with religious conviction, is that Being is and Not-being is not – which perhaps one can say, a little over-defining his meaning, means that all things are upheld by instress and are meaningless without it. . . . His feeling for instress, for the flush and foredrawn, and for inscape is most striking . . . (JP 127)

Hopkins is here picking up Parmenides' concern for one of the simplest and most profound of all philosophical questions. What is meant by saying that a thing *is*? or that it is *as* it is? Parmenides' answer was that Being *is* and Not-being *is not*: Hopkins adds his own gloss to this by saying that the matter is not so simple as that:

I have often felt when I have been in this mood and felt the depth of an instress or how fast the inscape holds a thing that nothing is so pregnant and straightforward to the truth as simple *yes* and *is*. 'Thou couldst never either know or say what was not, there would be no coming at it.' There would be no bridge, no stem of stress between us and things to bear us out and carry the mind over: . . . (JP 127)

Hopkins is here identifying two related qualities. One is *inscape*, 'how fast the inscape holds a thing', which seems to indicate the essence or substance of the thing which prevents it from changing into something else, holds it as it is. This quality is its 'inscape', that which gives it its own special and particular identity. 'Instress' is also present, as something which is *felt*: 'I have . . . felt the depth of an instress.' It seems to be that which exists deep within a thing and which is felt by the perceiving mind (which is how the mind knows that it *is*). It is not sufficient to say 'yes' and 'is' (this must be the meaning of the sentence 'nothing is so . . . straightforward . . . as simple *yes* and *is*'). How do we know that it is? We need stress or instress to carry over something deep within the object to somewhere deep within our own mind before we can 'know' it.

The words 'inscape' and 'instress' are therefore closely connected (a) with the world of physical things, and, indeed, mental and spiritual things too (inscape) and (b) with our perception of the external world and the forces within it (instress). They are essentially the processes which have to do with *realism*: Parmenides, Hopkins noted, was revered by Plato 'as the great father of Realism' (JP 127). Hopkins' own use of inscape and instress is concerned with his attempt to render the external world as accurately and vividly as possible.

To this must be added a later influence (1872), that of the medieval theologian and philosopher Duns Scotus. Scotus emphasized the distinctiveness of individual finite things, their determination into a specific form which he called *haecceitas* or 'thisness'. In particular Scotus, to Hopkins' delight, emphasized the activity of things, the way in which their individuality was demonstrated by what they did:

> *Each mortal thing does one thing and the same:*
> *Deals out that being indoors each one dwells;*
> *Selves — goes itself; myself it speaks and spells,*
> *Crying* Whát I dó is me: for that I came.
> 'As kingfishers catch fire . . .'

Long before his reading of Scotus, however, Hopkins had been conscious of the variety of individual appearances and the abundance of the created world. In 1866, for instance, we find journal entries such as this:

June 3. Showers, but mostly bright and hot. Clouds growing in beauty at end of the day. In the afternoon a white rack of two parallel spines, vertebrated as so often. At sunset, when the sky had charm and beauty. very level clouds, long pelleted sticks of shade-softened grey in the West. with gold-colour splashed sunset-spot, then more to the S. grey rows rather thicker and their oblique flake or thread better marked, . . . (JP 138)

The habit of noting things down truthfully and accurately came from a reading of Ruskin, whose *Modern Painters* would have encouraged

Hopkins in the observation of minute effects such as the movement of water behind a boat:

A barge, I find, not only wrinkles smooth water by a wedge outlined in parallel straight lap-waves but also, before and without these, shallower ones running, say midway, between those of the wedge and a perpendicular to the current. (JP 139)

Inscape is concerned with the way in which such things hold together in nature, in which they are themselves rather than anything else: so that an elm tree, for example, looks different from other trees. It has its own *haecceitas* or thisness, which might be described as an 'elm-ness' as opposed to an 'oak-ness' or a 'poplar-ness'. The inscape of an elm tree is the property by which we recognize it: but it is not just its shape or 'scape': it is its 'inscape', its inner being or self-hood, the thing itself in its own special nature. Not only is this individual essence found in the external world; it is found in each individual, who (in Hopkins' view) is to know his own individual self-hood and cultivate its distinctiveness. It is known in everything, in every tune in music, and in every poem. 'No doubt my poetry errs on the side of oddness,' wrote Hopkins to Bridges in 1879:

But as air, melody, is what strikes me most of all in music and design in painting, so design, pattern or what I am in the habit of calling 'inscape' is what I above all aim at in poetry. Now it is the virtue of design, pattern, or inscape to be distinctive and it is the vice of distinctiveness to become queer. This vice I cannot have escaped. (LB 66)

So each poem, like the creatures and things in 'As kingfishers catch fire . . .', speaks and spells *itself*: it selves. And if it is a vice to become queer, it is a virtue to be distinctive. Every one of Hopkins' poems is distinctive and unmistakable: none could have been written by anyone else, and each one has its own separate identity. Each has verbal, rhythmical, musical and other significant features which make it different from all other poems. In the same way, the inner features of anything in the universe have their own individuality, and this makes up the distinctiveness of each species or kind: so kingfishers (unlike any other birds) have the property of seeming to catch fire in their flight, and stones ring as they bounce against the sides of round wells. And the function of the poet must be not only to write poems which have their own inscape, but to remind people of the inscape of things. Writing in his journal for March 1871, Hopkins described the shaping of a cloud, and added, 'Unless you refresh the mind from time to time you cannot always remember or believe how deep the inscape in things is.' (JP 205)

33

Inscape is closely related to instress. In his journal for 22 April 1871, Hopkins wrote:

But such a lovely damasking in the sky as today I never felt before. The blue was charged with simple instress, the higher, zenith sky earnest and frowning, lower more light and sweet (JP 207).

In May of the previous year he had written:

May 18. Great brilliancy and projection: the eye seemed to fall perpendicular from level to level along our trees, the nearer and further Park; all things hitting the sense with double but direct instress (JP 199).

If inscape is the 'within-scape' of something, its inner shape, then it is probably correct to see instress as the 'within-stress' of a thing, the force or stress that comes from within something and which is felt by the beholder as 'stressing' it, giving it its stress from within itself. Instress is a force, and it is *felt*: if the inscape holds a thing, then it is the instress of the thing which is felt. This idea is extended beyond the things of this world to something as holy as the Godhead:

> *Since, tho' he is under the world's splendour and wonder,*
> *His mystery must be instressed, stressed;*
> *For I greet him the days I meet him, and bless when I understand.*
> 'Wreck', stanza 5

Mystery is the central instress of God (meaning 'mysterious' in the sense of holy, as well as beyond human understanding): it must be stressed, or emphasized, but it must also be instressed – that is, it must be the force which is felt by the believer, who blesses when he understands. As in so many of the things which Hopkins writes about, it has an external force and an internal one: together they make up the distinctiveness of a thing, its inscape and instress.

Sprung Rhythm

A good deal of pother is sometimes made about sprung rhythm. This is a pity, because it is not very difficult to understand; Hopkins himself believed that it was stronger and more natural than the customary metre of poetry, which counts a regular number of feet and syllables:

> *The curfew tolls the knell of parting day . . .*

This line requires ten syllables to be correct, with the emphasis usually falling on an iambic foot (two syllables, short–long). In Hopkins' view this led to an unnatural form of writing, and a weaker one, because unnecessary syllables often had to be put in to provide the correct number for the line. He wanted to be able to say in verse what he would normally say in prose:

why, if it is forcible in prose to say 'lashed rod', am I obliged to weaken this in verse, which ought to be stronger, not weaker, into 'lashed birch-rod' or something? (LB 46)

The two syllables together give an obviously powerful effect:

> *I did say yes*
> *O at lightning and lashed rod; . . .*
> 'Wreck', stanza 2

Sprung rhythm allows this kind of effect, and many others. Hopkins described it as follows:

To speak shortly, it consists in scanning by accents or stresses alone, without any account of the number of syllables, so that a foot may be one strong syllable or it may be many light and one strong (LD 14).

The examples which he gave were from nursery rhymes, 'Ding, dong, bell' and 'One, two buckle my shoe'; and if we write out the nursery rhyme and count its syllables, the point is clear:

Ding, dong, bell;	3
Pussy's in the well;	5
Who put her in?	4
Little Johnny Thin.	5
Who pulled her out?	4
Little Johnny Stout.	5

There are a varying number of syllables in each line, but the same three stresses. Hopkins thought, correctly, that this was closer to ordinary speech than most poetry – 'a better and more natural principle than the ordinary system – much more flexible, and capable of much greater effects' (LD 14–15).

In the 'Author's Preface' to his poems, Hopkins explains this as just an extension of what goes on in all poetry. Poets have a metrical scheme, and deviate from it to gain an effect: so that what goes on in the mind is an awareness of the original regular rhythm together with the deviation from it (Hopkins called this 'mounted rhythm' or 'counterpoint'):

the new or mounted rhythm is actually heard and at the same time the mind naturally supplies the natural or standard foregoing rhythm, for we do not forget what the rhythm is that by rights we should be hearing, two rhythms are in some manner running at once and we have something answerable to counterpoint in music, which is two or more strains of tune going on together... (Penguin edition, p. 8)

The next step is that the poet counterpoints throughout. But if he does so, then the original metre disappears completely, because it has never had a chance to become established. It is no longer one element in the counterpoint; and at this stage the metre that is left seems to be merely irregular:

if you counterpoint throughout, since one only of the counter rhythms is actually heard, the other is really destroyed or cannot come to exist, and what is written is one rhythm only and probably Sprung Rhythm ... (p. 9)

So Sprung Rhythm, like natural speech, makes its own patterns of sound: sometimes with a foot of one syllable, sometimes with two, up to four. So, in 'The Wreck of the Deutschland', there are monosyllabic feet:

Jésŭ, | heárt's | líght,

and ones with four syllables (known as 'paeons'):

Startlĕ thĕ poŏr | sheep băck! Ĭs thĕ | shĭpwrăck thĕn ă | hárvĕst, / doĕs | témpĕst cărry thĕ | graín for theĕ?

Throughout his 'Author's Preface' the reader is conscious of the fact that Hopkins was a musician as well as a poet. His metrical feet, however long, begin with a stressed syllable like the first beat of a bar; and he employs other musical marks:

namely accents, where the reader might be in doubt which syllable should have the stress; slurs, that is loops *over* syllables, to tie them together into the time of one; little loops at the end of a line to shew that the rhyme goes on to the first letter of the next line; what in music are called pauses . , to shew that the syllable should be dwelt on; and twirls ~ , to mark reversed or counterpointed rhythm (pp. 10–11).

Although sprung rhythm is close to natural speech, it is important to remember that for Hopkins there was always the unheard rhythm beneath, the regular metre which he was counterpointing. Otherwise the whole thing would become like prose; and Hopkins was such a severe self-disciplinarian that he required something more demanding. 'The Wreck of the Deutschland', for example, has a regular system of stresses in every stanza. On one of the manuscripts, Hopkins wrote:

Be pleased, reader, since the rhythm in which the following poem is new, strongly to mark the beats of the measure, according to the number belonging to each of the eight lines of the stanza, as the indentation guides the eye, namely two and three and four and three and five and five and four and six: ... laying on the beats too much stress rather than too little; not caring whether one, two, three or more syllables go to a beat ...

In fact the second part of the poem, from stanza 11 onwards, has *three* stresses on the first line of each stanza, not two. The following is a straightforward example:

> On Sáturday sáiled from Brémen,
> Américan-oútward-bóund,
> Take séttler and séaman, tell mén with wómen,
> Two húndred sóuls in the roúnd –
> O Fáther, not únder thy féathers nor éver as guéssing
> The góal was a shóal, of a foúrth the dóom to be drówned;
> Yet did the dárk síde of the báy of thy bléssing
> Not vaúlt them, the míllions of roúnds of thy mércy not reéve even thém
> in?

The stresses are, as Hopkins said, 3–3–4–3–5–5–4–6; and the lines are spaced from the left-hand margin accordingly, so that line 7, for instance, of four stresses, is indented beneath line 3, also of four stresses.

In this particular stanza, the strong stress at the end of line 6 ('drowned') enables a series of short syllables to begin line 7. This counters any tendency towards regularity with a natural connection from line to line:

it is natural in Sprung Rhythm for the lines to be *rove over*, that is for the scanning of each line immediately to take up that of the one before, so that if the first has one or more syllables at its end the other must have so many the less at its beginning; and in fact the scanning runs on without break from the beginning, say, of a stanza to the end and all the stanza is one long strain, though written in lines asunder. (p. 10)

Again, Hopkins is thinking musically ('all ... is one long strain'): a piece of music may have separate phrases, and be divided into bars, but the musical phrases are connected to one another and make a whole. Similarly the poems can (though rarely) have rests as in music: Hopkins gave as an example the second line of 'The Leaden Echo and the Golden Echo':

Back beauty, keep it, beauty, beauty, beauty, ... from vanishing away?

Such a rest, which causes the mind and senses to stay on the three words 'beauty, beauty, beauty' is one example, according to Hopkins, of 'licences' which were 'natural to Sprung Rhythm'. The others were *'hangers* or *outrides*, that is one, two, or three slack syllables added to a foot and not counting in the nominal scanning':

They are so called because they seem to hang below the line or ride forward or backward from it in another dimension than the line itself, according to a principle needless to explain here. These outriding half feet or hangers are marked by a loop underneath them, and plenty of them will be found. (p. 10)

Except, he might have added, in 'The Wreck of the Deutschland', where (as he pointed out to Bridges, LB 45) 'there are no outriding feet'. Elsewhere, he saw them as a feature of his verse, and marked them accordingly. They are somehow an 'extra' to the line, and are very confusing. In 'Hurrahing in Harvest', for instance, the poet wrote the first two lines as follows:

> *Summer ends now; now, barbarous in beauty, the stooks arise*
> *Around; up above, what wind-walks! what lovely behaviour*

The word 'barbarous' would normally be scanned as a dactyl ($-\smile\smile$), but Hopkins specifically suggested that it should not be:

Take notice that the outriding feet are not to be confused with dactyls or paeons, though sometimes the line might be scanned either way. The strong syllable in an outriding foot has always a great stress and after the outrider follows a short pause. The paeon is easier and more flowing.

The scanning should therefore be, I believe:

> *Súmmer | ends nŏw; nŏw,| bár   ĭn| beáutў, thĕ| stóoks ărĭse*
> *   barous*
> *Ā| round; ŭp ăb| óve, whăt| wind-   whăt| lóvelў bĕ| hávioŭr*
> *   walks!*

The easier and more flowing paeon is a metrical foot of four syllables, usually $-\smile\smile\smile$, known as a 'falling paeon'. Hopkins described 'The Windhover' as being in 'Falling paeonic rhythm, sprung and outriding', and marked the first three lines with stresses and outrides as follows:

> *I cáught this mórning mórning's mínion, kíng-*
> *   dom of dáylight's dáuphin, dapple-dáwn-drawn Fálcon, in his ríding*
> *   Of the rólling level underneath him steady aír, and stríding*

The scansion therefore appears to be:

38

I cáught thís | mórning | mórning's | minion, | kíng-
dŏm ŏf | dáyligh̆t's | dáu   *, dăpplĕ | dáwn-drăwn | Fãl*   *, ĭn hĭs |*
                    phin   *con*

rídĭng
Ŏf thĕ róll   *lĕvĕl | úndĕr | néath*   *stĕadў | aír, ănd strĭdĭng*
              ing   *him*

The lines are *rove over* conspicuously here, with each line's ending leading to the following one's stress or unstress. At the end of the third line, for example, the paeon 'air, and striding' leads to a marvellous stress at the opening of line 4 – 'High there'.

This scansion is not intended to be definitive: critics are wary about Hopkins' intentions and tend, prudently, to issue disclaimers. But it is close enough to suggest something of the rhythmical patterning and careful craftsmanship that goes into his poems. In particular, his use of sprung rhythm enables him to work flexibly within his own strict limits. It is not true to say that he can work 'freely', for he was always setting himself strict rules and conforming to strict patterns and demands. But the variation in the number of syllables, the natural rhythms of speech and prose, allow an extraordinary variety and liveliness in his work.

Hopkins' Poetic Language

In a letter to Robert Bridges, dated 4 January 1883, Hopkins briefly discussed the image of 'shook foil' in his poem 'God's Grandeur':

I mean foil in its sense of leaf or tinsel, and no other word whatever will give the effect I want. (LB 169)

'No other word whatever . . .': the sentence is absolutely precise and utterly uncompromising. It is typical of Hopkins to want to be so accurate; typical, too, of his sense of his craft. He made word-marks as a carver works in wood, as deliberately, purposefully and carefully. He had what can only be described as a passion for good language: his prose is uncluttered and expressive, his poetry rigorous in its pursuit of precision and exactness. He disliked pretentiousness and jargon, tired phrases, ugly formulations and bureaucratic vagueness:

This Victorian English is a bad business. They say 'It goes without saying' (and I wish it did) and instead of 'There is no such thing' they say a thing 'is non-existent' and *in* for *at* and *altruistic* and a lot more. (LB 284)

In contrast to this, Hopkins admired plain speech: 'I dearly love calling a

39

spade a spade', he wrote, and the reader feels that for once this is not a cliché or a pious hope. To Hopkins the word 'spade' was important, as the precise and unpretentious word used to signify a garden tool. At first sight, however, his poetry looks very different from this, as though he had decided to choose rare, unusual and striking words in preference to ordinary ones; but in fact its effects are often the result of trying to call a spade a spade, of trying to capture in word or phrase the exact essence or nature of something. In many cases, this involves seeing the object afresh, and Hopkins often assists with this by an unusual choice of words: his capacity for surprising the reader is enormous.

In the process of attempting to render something as exactly and freshly as possible, Hopkins uses an unusual and abundant vocabulary. His early diaries, even those written at school in 1863, show how interested he was in dialect words and in derivations:

Skim, scum, squama, scale, keel, (i.e. skeel) – *squama* and *scale* being the topmost flake what may be skimmed from surface of a thing. (JP 12)

Later he noted Irish expressions in his journals (JP 198–9), and loved to hear Lancashire people explaining their north-country words and phrases: 'Talking to James Shaw of Dutton Lee, who told us among other things that *lum* in Luke Lum means standing water and to *sail* as in Sail Wheel is to circle round' (JP 211); 'Robert says the first grass from the scythe is the *swathe*, then comes the *strow* (tedding), then *rowing*, then the footcocks, then *breaking*, then the *hubrows*, which are gathered into hubs . . .' (JP 212–13) In his poetry perhaps the most remarkable example of Lancashire usage is in 'Felix Randal':

> . . . *Ah well, God rest him all road ever he offended!*

where the word 'road' is from 'ony road' or 'any way', so that it can mean 'God rest (give him rest, forgive) him for all the ways in which he ever sinned'; or it can mean 'God rest him for his sins, anyway' (any road, all road, is still used to mean 'anyway' in East Lancashire); or it could possibly have a residual meaning of 'road' itself – 'God forgive him for his sins on all the roads he ever travelled and sinned on in the journey of life'. Other examples of dialect words include:

wuthering = wind blowing among trees ('Henry Purcell', from Yorkshire)
voel = hill ('Wreck', from Welsh)
degged = sprinkled ('Inversnaid', from Lancashire)
throng = crowded ('Ribblesdale', from Lancashire)
fashed = troubled ('The Leaden Echo . . .', from Scots)
throughther = through and together ('Spelt from Sibyl's Leaves', from Scots)

An adjective turned verb is 'sour'

> ... *before it cloy,*
> *Before it cloud, Christ, lord, and sour with sinning.*
> 'Spring'

Here the sound of 'cloy' leads on to 'cloud', which means 'to go cloudy' (as a clear liquid goes cloudy). It is a good example of the way in which the meaning of one word complements and expands the meaning of another. Words give rise to other, similar words, either through assonance, alliteration or echo. Rhyming words, in particular, stir up ideas in an unexpectedly vivid way. To say of the *Deutschland*, for example, that 'The goal was a shoal' seems shocking and almost absurd; yet the phrase intensifies the way the ship drives onwards towards the sandbank, as if aiming for it. Another example of such intensification of meaning comes in 'frightful a nightfall' ('Wreck', stanza 15): the juxtaposition of the two words seems to underline them both. Similarly in 'The Windhover'

> *My heart in hiding*
> *Stirred for a bird, ...*

suggests the connection between the two, the leaping heart and the flying bird. Sometimes the internal rhyming seems to be playful

> *Not spared, not one*
> *That dandled a sandalled*
> *Shadow that swam or sank ...*
> 'Binsey Poplars'

but the playfulness is undercut by the awareness that this is in the past, that the poplars have been 'felled, felled, ...' In the same poem, 'Binsey Poplars', human beings 'Hack and rack the growing green!' (cut it about and torture it) and where they intend 'To mend her we end her'. One sound gives rise to another: here the contrast between 'mend her' and 'end her' indicates the great gap between the intention and the result. The obtrusive rhyme holds not a similarity but a dissimilarity: the result is a strange concord and discord in the mind, a concordance of rhyming sound against a discordant meaning. In the process, however, the important thing is that the meanings get themselves noticed, become unusual, fresh and new, and are no longer stale with familiarity.

In addition to rhymes, there are half-rhymes, which echo but change the sound:

41

> *Now burn, new born to the world,*
> 'Wreck', stanza 34

> *Night roared, with the heart-break hearing a heart-broke rabble,*
> 'Wreck', stanza 17

and sometimes this echo of sound is used when Hopkins plays noun against verb:

> *Mark, the mark is of man's make*
> 'Wreck', stanza 22

Here 'mark' is first a verb in the imperative ('Mark!') and then a noun, which is echoed by 'make' later in the line. The reading of such a line requires extra attention: it has the facility of assonance and alliteration, but the reader has to disentangle the meaning from the similar sounds. Often these sounds cluster together in a kind of profusion:

> *In crisps of curl off wild winch whirl,* ...
> 'The Sea and the Skylark'

This is the lark's song, curling crisply, and whirling as a skein off a winch or bobbin that is going round wildly.

The unusual choice of words is further assisted by Hopkins' invention of his own compound words. Sometimes these are made up of noun plus noun, as in 'heavengravel', 'wolfsnow' and 'deathgush', all from 'The Loss of the Eurydice'. Sometimes there are adjectives joined to nouns, as 'gaygear' ('The Leaden Echo...') or 'hoarlight' ('Spelt from Sibyl's Leaves'), or 'earl-stars' suggesting both 'early stars' and 'major stars', and sandwiched between two such supporters (bringing out the meaning):

> ... *her earliest stars, earl-stars,' stárs principal* ...
> '... Sibyl's Leaves'

'Harry Ploughman' has a similarly remarkable line, with two compounds:

> *Churlsgrace, too, child of Amansstrength,*

which Hopkins uses to try to capture the mixture of grace and strength in the ploughman as he works.

Other words are rare because they are old-fashioned or obsolete, such as

reave = strip away ('Ribblesdale', 'Peace')
cogged = loaded ('The Leaden Echo...')

round = whisper ('Inversnaid')
mealed = mingled ('The Starlight Night')

and others occur only rarely in English prose or poetry (sometimes in Shakespeare, whose coinages Hopkins admired greatly):

sillion = furrow ('The Windhover')
rivelled = wrinkled ('Eurydice', from Shakespeare, *Troilus and Cressida*)
footing it = placing the feet ('The Caged Skylark', from Shakespeare, *The Tempest*).

He uses words which are often extremely unexpected in their context. Thus in 'Felix Randal' the poet imagines the blacksmith shoeing a horse with 'his bright and battering sandal'. A sandal is a protection for the sole of the foot, and a bright sandal shines; a battering sandal is a sole-covering that makes a battering noise as it hits the ground. So by the use of the unexpected word, Hopkins has drawn attention to the properties of the horseshoe that he is describing.

The life which this kind of process gives to Hopkins' poetry comes from a recognition that the unexpected word often makes the reader see an object afresh. As an extension of this, words are often found in unusual relationships with one another: nouns turn into adjectives, adjectives into nouns or verbs. The word 'throng', in 'Ribblesdale', for example, is usually a verb, but as Hopkins noted he was using it 'for an adjective as we use it here in Lancashire' (LD 109). Since the poem is about Lancashire this has a certain appropriateness, as though the voice which is describing the valley of the Ribble is a local voice. Another example is 'burly' in 'The Wreck of the Deutschland', stanza 27:

> *. . . in wind's burly and beat of endragonèd seas.*

Some poems have more compounds than others: 'The Bugler's First Communion', for example, has 'bloomfall', 'backwheels', 'mansex', and 'The Loss of the Eurydice' has a great many too. Hopkins uses such words to fuse together different things, to produce a new idea which is a compression of two earlier ideas. With the use of hyphens he can compress a number of ideas tightly into place, as in the description of Christ in 'The Wreck of the Deutschland':

> *Doubled-naturèd name,*
> *The heaven-flung, heart-fleshed, maiden-furled*
> *Miracle-in-Mary-of-flame,*
> *Mid-numberèd He in three of the thunder-throne!*
>
> stanza 34

On another occasion, in 'Binsey Poplars', the compounds can be used to lengthen the picture, stretch it out like the line of a river-bank:

> *On meadow and river and wind-wandering weed-winding bank.*

Hopkins will often give life to ordinary words by using them in an unexpected metaphorical manner. The drowned seaman, in 'The Loss of the Eurydice', 'is strung by duty': that is, his body is un-flabby in the way that a tennis racket is taut when properly strung. In 'Spring' –

> *The glassy peartree leaves and blooms, they brush*
> *The descending blue; that blue is all in a rush*
> *With richness;*

and here the leaves shine like glass; they seem to brush the sky, like a paintbrush touching a canvas. The sky itself is 'the blue', 'that blue', a metonymy which takes the colour alone and uses it to describe the whole sky. Such an economy is typical: in 'The Windhover' Hopkins does not require the final syllable of the word 'achievement', which would weaken the line by a moment which does not mean much, so he writes 'the achieve of, the mastery of the thing!' At other times, unexpected words enrich the meaning, as in 'The Wreck of the Deutschland', where Hopkins makes a verb from the noun for a Christian festival – 'Let him easter in us'. It would have been quite possible, though conventional, to say 'let him rise within us', but the new verb carried all the connotations of the mysterious and miraculous resurrection. Similarly, in 'As kingfishers catch fire . . .', he invents a word – 'selves' – which saves him from the usual expressions: each mortal thing 'selves', that is, declares itself, is itself, is being, and in being is itself.

In all these tricks and devices of vocabulary, Hopkins can be seen to be choosing his words very carefully, getting the most out of every phrase and every line. Each poem has its own kind of distinct decorum too, so that the linguistic devices of one are not appropriate for another. Some are complex and intricate, some full of repetition, some intense, some simple. In each case, Hopkins is looking for the word which will fit into the poem and describe the object most precisely and exactly. An example of his concern may be found in a letter to Bridges about 'Henry Purcell', and in particular about the words

> *only I'll*
> *Have an eye to the sakes of him . . .:*

Sake is a word I find it convenient to use: I did not know when I did so first that it is common in German, in the form *sach*. It is the *sake* of 'for the sake of', *forsake*, *namesake, keepsake.* I mean by it the being a thing has outside itself, as a voice by its echo, a face by its reflection, a body by its shadow, a man by his name, fame, or memory, *and also* that in the thing by virtue of which especially it has this being abroad, and that is something distinctive, marked, specifically or individually speaking, as for a voice and echo clearness; for a reflected image light, brightness; for a shadow-casting body bulk; for a man genius, great achievements, amiability, and so on. (LB 83)

Hopkins often isolates a *part* of a word such as this: it is part of his acute observation of linguistic features in the language, and a desire to use them to the full.

The vocabulary of Hopkins' poetry is thus extremely interesting and individual. However, its full significance can be appreciated only in relation to other words, to the placing of the words within the line, to the metrics and to the construction of the poem as a whole. Here Hopkins' art is even more remarkable for its constructions, its omissions, its inversions, its tempo and its sound.

It is often the constructions and inversions which have given most difficulty. Coventry Patmore, Hopkins' contemporary, described Hopkins' poetry as 'veins of pure gold embedded in masses of impracticable quartz' (letter to Robert Bridges, 2 May 1884), which suggests that he saw individual images and perceptions as surrounded by confusing and difficult grammatical forms. But as the vocabulary was aiming at exactness, so too the different formations of phrase, line and sentence structure were also intended to produce an exact effect in the mind of the reader. When Hopkins provides an unusual construction or a strange image, he usually has a reason for it: after all, he is quite capable of writing (as he usually does in prose) with a lucid simplicity. Examples may be found in 'Pied Beauty', or the first line of 'Spring' or of 'God's Grandeur'. But in other places the syntax seems to be twisted into strange shapes:

> *Recorded only, I have put my lips on pleas*
> *Would brandle adamantine heaven with ride and jar, did*
> > *Prayer go disregarded: . . .*
> > > 'The Bugler's First Communion'

Hopkins knows that he cannot compel the boy to remain good and faithful; that he must leave to God. But he wants to put it on record that he has prayed such prayers that, if they were disregarded, they would shake ('brandle') heaven. Another time Hopkins will use a Germanic construction, with the verb at the end:

> *why must*
> *Disappointment all I endeavour end?*
> 'Thou art indeed just, Lord . . .'

The sentence structure allows full weight to be given to 'disappointment', and gives the echo '*end*-eavour *end*', while putting 'end' as the final word in the sentence and in the line helps to enact its finality. This use of words to represent the feel of emotion and idea is a fundamental feature of Hopkins' poetic art:

> *O the mind, mind has mountains; cliffs of fall*
> *Frightful, sheer, no-man-fathomed. Hold them cheap*
> *May who ne'er hung there.*
> 'No worst, there is none . . .'

Here the beat of the words is vitally important, for the stresses hold the meaning: 'O the mind, mind' becomes not just a statement but an exclamation, with the repetition deepening the concentration. Then comes the surprise: the mind 'has mountains'. The change from mind to mountain is very sharp and sudden; and no sooner has the reader tried to adjust to this inner landscape than it is opposed and expanded by the phrase 'cliffs of fall'. These are not mountains or cliffs to be looked up at, but precipices to be fallen down, and the 'fall' comes at the end of the line, so that the reader's mind has to hold it for a split second before dropping to the next line: there is, for a moment, nothing to 'hold on to' except adjectives, two ordinary ones and one compound one:

> *Frightful, sheer, no-man-fathomed.*

At the full stop, the reader hits bottom: the syllables have been succeeding one another at great speed, and the 'no-man-fathomed' actually forces an acceleration, as if falling through the air. Then comes another surprising twist:

> *Hold them cheap*
> *May who ne'er hung there.*

The contrast between the physically felt cliff-falls of the mind, and 'Hold them cheap' could hardly be stronger. The first suggests a frightening instability, the second a securely-based judgment. The explanation comes all the more forcefully because it has been held back: 'May who ne'er hung there'. 'We may', argues the poet, 'have little respect for those who have not experienced the heights and depths, the mountains and precipices of the mind'; but the word 'hung' suggests the urgency and the

immediacy, the pain and the tension, of such a situation, so that even
'Hold them cheap' starts with an equilibrium and finishes with a poised
crisis. What follows is still stranger:

> *Nor does long our small*
> *Durance deal with that steep or deep.*

What Hopkins is saying is that we cannot endure such tension for any
length of time; but he twists this about, so that five words at the end of
the line have little meaning until they are completed by the unusual and
strong word 'Durance' (endurance: as with 'achieve', Hopkins has
dropped a weak syllable). 'Small Durance' is almost a contradiction in
terms, and certainly seems inadequate (as Hopkins intended) to deal
with what follows, the 'steep or deep' of the mind. As so often in Hopkins,
these words chime, the sounds acting against the direct opposition and
giving rise to 'creep' further on in the line:

> *Here! creep,*
> *Wretch, under a comfort serves in a whirlwind:*

The images of mountain and cliff have now given way to the imagery of
storm, or rather reverted to it, for it was found at the beginning of the
sonnet. In both the cliff description and the storm description, Hopkins
finds extremely powerful physical expressions to denote mental processes
and moods; and this physical imagery is reinforced by the speech-needs
of the lines, which require a corresponding effort in speaking or even
reading them (chiefly because of the twists and turns of the syntax and
sentence-structure).

This sense of physical effort is extremely strong in Hopkins, especially
in his descriptions of religious struggle or crisis, such as stanza 2 of 'The
Wreck of the Deutschland'. Its opposite is found in the light-moving
delicacy of some of the descriptions of nature and beauty. In each case,
Hopkins is able to find words that express the physical in language, and
the spiritual in physical. He was very interested in what might be called
the physical way of speaking, as in his description of two Lancashire
gardeners:

It is so funny to hear the people of this country saying Ay. Our two gardeners, for
instance are often talking over their work. They are shy of being overheard but
they cannot conceal their agreements. What the one says the other assents to by
the roots and upwards from the level of the sea. He makes a kind of Etna of
assent, without effort but with a long fervent breathing out of all the breath that
is in him. The word runs through the whole scale of the vowels beginning broad
in the barrel of the waist and ending fine on the drop of the lip. (FL 113–14)

47

In something of the same way, Hopkins' own mental and poetical (not to mention spiritual) life existed in a way which involved body as well as mind and spirit. His poetry *feels after* the thing described, using the rhythms and stresses, the line-endings and beginnings, to produce something of the same struggle, or the same smoothness or lightness, in the reader's mind. His alterations in word-order are therefore purposeful, for they often have the effect of throwing the stress exactly on the point where it is required. A good example is the description of Divine Providence in 'The Wreck of the Deutschland':

> *lovely-felicitous Providence*
> *Finger of a tender of, O of a feathery delicacy, the breast of the*
> *Maiden could obey so, be a bell to, ring of it, and*
> *Startle the poor sheep back!*

Here the stresses and sounds produce an extraordinary combination with the meanings: the intricate confusions of phrase, the interruptions of the sense, the half-completed sentences, all contribute to the effect which Hopkins desires to produce. He is looking, principally, towards the strategically-placed verb, the all-important 'Startle', which has a tremendous effect at the beginning of the line. He is arguing that God's Providence is there for the 'comfortless unconfessed of them' in the storm, through the presence and example of the nun ('the Maiden'); this presence is like a bell to the sheep to startle them back into the fold. The image of the lost sheep is a very common one: now they are to be 'startled' back by a sudden realization of the crisis and the nun's behaviour in it. That behaviour, we could say, 'rings true'. It 'rings' the note of God's Providence, which is not a heavy or slow or mechanical thing but 'lovely-felicitous Providence': the compound adjective with all its syllables suggests a nimble, quick-moving thing. Then it becomes 'of a feathery delicacy', which seems to pick up the rapid movement of 'lovely-felicitous'. It is the delicacy of God's Providence that the nun obeys, and in obeying she is a reminder to others of it (she is a 'bell' to it).

So the whole passage has to be reshaped to make sense in prose, thus losing all its tension. We could say, for instance, that the poet was celebrating

the finger of a tender lovely-felicitous Providence, that Providence of a feathery delicacy which the breast of the maiden could so obey, could be to it such a bell, that it would startle the poor sheep back into the fold.

This summary is still somewhat confusing, and a further paraphrase would probably say that 'God's providence is wonderful in its delicacy and grace, which provides the nun at the right moment to show the power of His Grace, and startle (not just bring) the lost sheep back into the fold.' But the simpler we make the poem, the more we paraphrase, the further we get from Hopkins.

The strong sense of interconnecting lines between words, and the relationship between different parts of a line and different words in a line, is extremely important in Hopkins. So too is alliteration. In all these things he was strongly influenced by his slight acquaintance with Welsh poetry. In particular, the highly-developed system of alliteration, syllable-number, and rhyme, known as *Cynghanedd*, drew his attention not just to words that began with the same letter but to a more strict kind of alliteration. In some forms of Cynghanedd, words of two or more syllables alliterate only when all their consonants except the last are the same, and in the same order (thus 'moonlight' alliterates with 'manly', and 'manners' with 'money'). The stresses must be the same ('sorrow' can alliterate with 'serious' but not with 'serene') and groups of words can alliterate ('hide thy face' with 'heed the fire'). So in Hopkins we have

> *Warm-laid grave of a womb-life grey;*
> 'Wreck', stanza 7

There are many different kinds of Cynghanedd, and it is not difficult to see why some of them attracted Hopkins. They produce patterns of sound, both of consonant and vowel, and in Hopkins' use of it this often adds to the sense in surprising and original ways. In one of the Cynghaneddion, for example, the *Draws*, the first part of the line alliterates with the last part, with a portion in the middle of the line that is traversed or passed over. So in Hopkins there is

> *The keener to come at the comfort for feeling the combating keen?*
> 'Wreck', stanza 25

Here Hopkins has added his own chiasmus, the a–b–b–a structure of 'keener – come – combating – keen'. Another example of alliteration with the middle passed over is 'Ten or twelve, only ten or twelve' ('Binsey Poplars'); at other times the alliteration draws attention to the different vowel-sounds of the words, so that the words themselves are seen anew:

> *That piecemeal peace is poor peace. What pure peace allows*
> 'Peace'

49

Such effects may have been influenced by the different forms of Cynghanedd, but of course Hopkins uses them for his own purposes. Nevertheless, it is clear that he was attracted by the Welsh strict metres, possibly because of their sheer intricacy and difficulty: they satisfied the need of the craftsman within him to set himself problems and solve them. And when, in the solving, he was able to produce unexpected beauties and delights, the possibilities became even more attractive.

In the use of such vowel and consonant sounds, it is evident that Hopkins thought of poetry as 'speech', and he was very clear about the importance of both sound and rhythm. 'Poetry is speech framed for contemplation of the mind by the way of hearing or speech framed to be heard for its own sake and interest even over and above its interest of meaning' (J P 289). Again and again his notes suggest that the poems are to be *spoken*, not read: 'Harry Ploughman', for instance, 'is altogether for recital, and not for perusal (as by nature verse should be)' (LB 263), and 'Spelt from Sibyl's Leaves' is similarly described:

Of this long sonnet above all remember what applies to all my verse, that it is, as living art should be, made for performance and that its performance is not reading with the eye but loud, leisurely, poetical (not rhetorical) recitation, with long rests, long dwells on the rhyme and other marked syllables, and so on. This sonnet shd. be almost sung: it is most carefully timed in *tempo rubato*. (LB 246)

The last direction is yet another reminder that Hopkins was a musician, and that musical effects were often in his mind *(tempo rubato* means 'flexible time').

In addition to this idea that poetry is speech, with a musical tempo, it must also be noted that Hopkins described it as 'speech framed'. As a picture is framed, so a poem is speech with its specific edges and borders: it has a predetermined number of lines (there is evidence, for example, that Hopkins thought a great deal about sonnet form) or a verse form, or a pattern of stresses. One difference between poetry and speech is that poetry has its form, however flexible that may be; and in Hopkins' case he paid considerable attention to formal qualities, especially to the correctness of rhymes and the proper observance of rhythmical patterns. Even when he deviated from normal rhythms by the use of sprung rhythm and outriding syllables, he was always aware of the exact rhythm from which he was swerving. Sometimes the lines have a musical pattern of pause and acceleration, like rests and semi-quavers in a line of music:

Finger of a tender of, O of a feathery delicacy, the breast of the
'Wreck', stanza 31

Much of Hopkins' work shows such a musical sense; and above all it should be remembered that his unusual devices are always there for a purpose. The principal ones may be summarized as follows:

1. The use of alliteration. In Hopkins this is extremely interesting: it is found everywhere in his poetry but it rarely becomes tiresome because it is used in a most illuminating and original manner. Often the initial consonant gives rise to another word and another thought in Hopkins' mind, as one word develops another idea:

> *My aspens dear, whose airy cages quelled,*
> *Quelled or quenched in leaves the leaping sun,*
> 'Binsey Poplars'

> *And canvas and compass, the whorl and the wheel*
> 'Wreck', stanza 14

> *The cross to her she calls Christ to her, . . .*
> 'Wreck', stanza 24

> *. . . it is all a purchase, all is a prize.*
> 'The Starlight Night'

> *Thy river, and o'er gives all to rack and wrong.*
> 'Ribblesdale'

2. Assonance. This occurs when the correspondence of vowel sound is the same, or nearly the same, or when one word chimes with another. Hopkins uses it a great deal, and was very interested in rhymes, to which he applied strict rules and principles. A spectacular example of chiming assonance is found in 'As kingfishers catch fire . . .':

> *Stones ring; like each tucked string tells, each hung bell's*
> *Bow swung finds tongue to fling out broad its name;*
> *Each mortal thing does one thing and the same;*

Here the '-ing' and '-ung' sounds obviously enact the sound of the bells, counterbalanced by 'tells . . . bells', and the great stress on 'broad'. So too the line from 'God's Grandeur':

> *And all is seared with trade; bleared, smeared with toil*

uses the '-ea' sound to link the three verbs of spoiling.

3. The use of repetition. This is necessarily linked to alliteration and assonance, because if a word is repeated it has the same sound. Hopkins repeats words in order to deepen their emotional effect:

> *O the mind, mind has mountains;*
>   'No worst, there is none . . .'

>   *not live this tormented mind*
>   *With this tormented mind tormenting yet.*
>   'My own heart . . .'

Such repetition sets up echoes, and is naturally used in 'The Leaden Echo and the Golden Echo', where the leaden echo ends

>   *Be beginning to despair, to despair,*
>   *Despair, despair, despair, despair.*

and the golden echo ends

>   *We follow, now we follow. –*
>   *Yonder, yes yonder, yonder,*
>   *Yonder.*

Often, as in the first example in this section, the repetition causes a pause, and a swing in the line:

>   *this bids wear*
>   *Earth brows of such care, care and dear concern.*

This is a trick which Hopkins caught from Shakespeare, in *The Winter's Tale* IV. iv.: 'Move still, still so' (one of many examples of the influence of Shakespeare's language in Hopkins' poetry).

4. Repetition with expansion. In this figure, Hopkins makes a statement, takes a breath, and then amplifies the first statement:

>   *. . . but be adored, but be adored King.*
>   'Wreck', stanza 10

>   *. . . his nest,*
>   *But his own nest, wild nest, . . .*
>   'The Caged Skylark'

>   *What hours, O what black hours . . .*
>   'I wake and feel . . .'

>   *When, when, Peace, will you, Peace?*
>   'Peace'

As has been noted above, different poems have different degrees of repetition: a poem such as 'Binsey Poplars', for instance, has many chimes and repetitions. Hopkins himself noted 'certain chimes suggested by the Welsh poetry I had been reading (what they call *cynghanedd*)', in a letter to Dixon (LD 15).

5. The use of internal rhyme (discussed above):

> *All the air things wear ...*
> 'In the Valley of the Elwy'

> *In coop and in comb the fleece of his foam*
> 'Inversnaid'

6. The use of chiasmus (a–b–b–a), often with a slight shift in the second part, producing an effect which is almost symmetrical but not quite:

> *To seem the stranger lies my lot, my life*
> *Among strangers.*
> 'To seem the stranger ...'

> *Thy lovely dale down thus and thus bids reel*
> *Thy river,*
> 'Ribblesdale'

> *Make mercy in all of us, out of us all*
> *Mastery,*
> 'Wreck', stanza 10

> *This seeing the sick endears them to us, us too it endears.*
> 'Felix Randal'

> *That piecemeal peace is poor peace. What pure peace allows*
> 'Peace'

7. The use of phrases or compounds which repeat constructions. This often gives the poetry something of a rhetorical feel:

> *As kingfishers catch fire, dragonflies draw flame;*
> 'As kingfishers catch fire ...'

> *Cuckoo-echoing, bell-swarmèd, lark-charmèd, rook-racked, river-rounded;*
> 'Duns Scotus's Oxford'

> *What is all this juice and all this joy?*
> 'Spring'

> *There | God to aggrándise, God to glorify –*
> 'The Candle Indoors'

8. The use of inversion. This often produces a tension in the reader because of the unexpected word order; sometimes this is a pleasing tension, a bracing of the phrase which makes it feel different from prose and more expressive:

> *has wilder, wilful-wavier*
> *Meal-drift moulded ever and melted across skies?*
> 'Hurrahing in Harvest'

at other times it is expressive of an emotional tension in the poet which is severe and demanding:

> *why must*
> *Disappointment all I endeavour end?*
> 'Thou art indeed just, Lord . . .'

Such a use of constructions to convey emotion is part of a complex art in which Hopkins' poetic language is powerfully expressive of the ebb and flow of emotion. This is shown, very clearly in the way in which he uses the exclamation 'O' or 'Oh':

9. The expressive pause, with exclamation:

> *Finger of a tender of, O of a feathery delicacy,*
> 'Wreck', stanza 31

> *Brute beauty and valour and act, oh, air, pride, plume, here*
> 'The Windhover'

> *And hurls for him, O half hurls earth for him off under his feet.*
> 'Hurrahing in Harvest'

> *Complete thy creature dear O where it fails,*
> 'In the Valley of the Elwy'

> *England whose honour O all my heart woos, wife*
> 'To seem the stranger . . .'

This habit is so common that examples can be found everywhere. Its exclamatory quality is associated with:

10. The large number of question marks and exclamation marks. As with other devices, this is associated with speech, and notably with direct speech in a state of excitement. So Hopkins' enthusiasm often shows itself in lines such as

> *Let him oh! with his air of angels then lift me, lay me!*
> 'Henry Purcell'

> *Buy then! bid then! – What? – Prayer, patience, alms, vows.*
> 'The Starlight Night'

> *Thou mastering me*
> *God!*
> 'Wreck', stanza 1

There are so many of these exclamation marks, often in the middle of lines, that there is, again, no shortage of examples. Similarly, though not quite so frequently, Hopkins uses question marks to create a kind of active or dramatic situation, with question and answer:

> *What would the world be, once bereft*
> *Of wet and of wilderness?*
> 'Inversnaid'

> *And what is Earth's eye, tongue, or heart else, where*
> *Else, but in dear and dogged man?*
> 'Ribblesdale'

These are both questions addressed to a large audience, inviting all readers to reflect. At other times Hopkins addresses God with a question from the Old Testament:

> *Why do sinners' ways prosper? and why must*
> *Disappointment all I endeavour end?*
> 'Thou art indeed just, Lord . . .'

or he asks a dramatic question:

> *The frown of his face*
> *Before me, the hurtle of hell*
> *Behind, where, where was a, where was a place?*
> 'Wreck', stanza 3

These expressive punctuation marks are often associated with
11. Hopkins' use of interjections. Like Browning (whom he thought coarse) Hopkins is often colloquial and energetically abrupt

> *Ah, touched in your bower of bone*
> *Are you! turned for an exquisite smart,*
> *Have you!*
> 'Wreck', stanza 18

> *Ah well! it is all a purchase, all is a prize.*
> 'The Starlight Night'

> *all were good*
> *To me, God knows, deserving no such thing:*
> 'In the Valley of the Elwy'

This is often allied to:

12. The use of parenthesis, often confusing because unmarked. In 'Patience, hard thing! . . .', for example:

> *Patience who asks*
> *Wants war, wants wounds; weary his times, his tasks;*
> *To do without, take tosses, and obey.*

Here the middle line is a parenthesis, and would be read more easily if it had brackets round it. Similarly, in 'My own heart let me more have pity on . . .', we hear of God

> *whose smile*
> *'s not wrung, see you; unforeseen times rather – as skies*
> *Betweenpie mountains – lights a lovely mile.*

Here the parenthesis is marked by dashes: but the passage is remarkable also for its exclamation ('see you', like Welsh 'look you') and for the extraordinary compound 'betweenpie' (see below, pp. 122–3). Among other linguistic devices we may note the use of zeugma (or 'yoke'), in which one verb does duty for more than one noun:

> *Man, how fast his firedint, ' his mark on mind, is gone!*
> 'That Nature is a Heraclitean Fire . . .'

and the use of *kennings*. A kenning is a roundabout way of describing something, much used in Old Norse poetry, through combining its attributes into a word (a ship as an 'oar-steed'). So Hopkins will describe a horseshoe as a 'bright and battering sandal' ('Felix Randal') and a stream bed as a 'rollrock highroad' ('Inversnaid'). There are many instances of this in Hopkins, and they enliven his poetry by making the reader see the object afresh.

Hopkins' language repays careful study: in addition to James Milroy's admirable book, *The Language of Gerard Manley Hopkins*, there is also F. R. Leavis's fine chapter on Hopkins in *New Bearings in English Poetry*. What Leavis claims is that Hopkins' language, while full of the devices which have been mentioned above, is actually closer to living speech than most poetry, and that in this respect he is like Shakespeare. Both poets demand to be read aloud: and Leavis is quite right when he points to Hopkins' frequent instruction that his poetry should be read 'with the ears'. Leavis adds 'and with the brains and the body', which is also right: Hopkins again and again writes poetry to which we respond physically, with the breath, the ears and the senses. To this end his language pushes normal poetic practice to its limits, and (paradoxically) makes us feel that somehow it is more natural and alive.

Hopkins' sonnet forms

Hopkins wrote so many of his shorter poems in sonnet form that it is helpful to have some understanding of the form itself and of Hopkins' variations upon it.

The basic form which he uses is that of the Petrarchan or Italian sonnet. This is fourteen lines long, and is divided into an *octave* (the first eight lines, rhyming ABBA ABBA) and a *sestet* (the last six lines, rhyming in various ways: the commonest in Hopkins is the very demanding CD CD CD; in 'Felix Randal', 'Ribblesdale', and 'To What Serves Mortal Beauty' he uses CCD CCD, also demanding; neither uses a fifth rhyme).

Hopkins was very interested in the *proportions* of a sonnet, the ratio of 8:6 in a unit of 14. He plays numerous variations upon it. 'Pied Beauty' and 'Peace' are what Hopkins called 'Curtal-Sonnets', constructed on the ratio 6:4 instead of 8:6, but with a 'halfline tailpiece'. 'Tom's Garland' and 'That Nature is a Heraclitean Fire' are sonnets with *codas* (end-pieces) which allow an extension of the thought and idea beyond the constriction of fourteen lines. Apart from these, it is instructive to see how disciplined Hopkins is in his use of rhyme and careful observance of poetic form: it was no doubt part of his temperamental need to be strict with himself, and he was as demanding in his choice of poetic mode as he was in his choice of a religious life.

4. The Great Dragon: 'The Wreck of the Deutschland'

In his note to 'The Wreck of the Deutschland', on its first publication, Robert Bridges described it as being 'like a great dragon folded in the gate to forbid all entrance'.

It is certainly a complex poem, theologically as well as technically. But it is Hopkins' longest, his major poem: it was written after a long period of self-imposed silence, and it contains his thought and his poetic manner in a particularly pure form. An examination of its expression and ideas is therefore an excellent base for the discovery of the shorter poems; and there is also something to be said for taking first a poem which was the first expression of Hopkins' mature years, the poem in which his individuality first became fully articulated in verse.

To read the opening of 'The Wreck of the Deutschland' is like opening the door on a gale. The energy which is created by the first four words, by their relationship with each other, and by their placing within the lines, is overwhelming:

> *Thou mastering me*
> *God!*

The first line is an amazing construction: it begins and ends with the pronouns 'Thou' and 'me', poised at either end of the line in all their simplicity and opposition: they stand for the *other* and for the *self*, that which is *me* and that which is *not me*. Placed as they are, they seem oddly isolated, alone: the 'Thou' arrives in the poem as the first word, and the reader has no idea who is being referred to. Similarly the 'me' is thrown down without any preliminary, so that the two pronouns seem oddly isolated: they exist in limbo, ready to fly off in any direction, as if they might pull the poetic line apart by their straight opposition. They are held together, of course, by the three-syllabled word 'mastering', so different from the stark monosyllables before and after it. That word 'mastering' acts as a tie, a syllabic rope holding together the different parts of the line; it has a centralizing force, just as the two outer words have a diffusive one. Then, because it is held back until the second line, the word 'God!' enters with tremendous force: it completes the incomplete sense of the first line, and because it is placed at the beginning of the line the reader comes down upon it with a great thump. It explains that the 'Thou' of the first line is God, the other, mastering me, myself, the human being: and nothing else is permitted to intervene in the encounter.

So at first sight, these four words appear to be a simple statement of interaction between the self and the other, between the human and the divine, between the immediate and the remote; it is then that we realize what complexity exists in the word 'mastering', the connecting word between the two utterly irreconcilable and different forces. God 'mastering' man could have a number of meanings:

God as master in the sense of owner: God as master, man as slave;
God as master in the sense of victor in a struggle: God as conqueror over man, who submits to Him;
God as master in the sense of master of a ship: God as owner, figure in charge;
God as master in the sense of teacher: God as master, man as pupil.

In all these ways 'Thou mastering me / God!' accumulates meanings and reverberations: the simplicity of 'Thou' and 'me' is tied by an intricate and many-stranded cord, which emphasizes throughout the power and mastery of God and the submissiveness of man. God's mastery and God's mystery are two of the fundamental assumptions of the poem, together with a realization of God's mercy.

The actual story of the shipwreck, which Hopkins had read in the newspapers, is therefore contained within a complex framework of ideas. It can be seen as beginning with the dedication and the title:

THE WRECK
OF THE DEUTSCHLAND

To the
happy memory of five Franciscan Nuns
exiles by the Falck Laws
drowned between midnight and morning of
Dec. 7th, 1875

The poem is about a shipwreck, a terrible event: it has its appalling side as five nuns, presumably five among many passengers, were drowned during the night. Those nuns were the victims of religious persecution, laws of Lutheran Germany from which they were fleeing (from Deutschland in the *Deutschland*, a savage coincidence that Hopkins notes and later makes use of). By contrast with their drowning, however, is their happy memory: even in the dedication Hopkins has begun to complicate the tragedy with religious considerations.

The happy memory of the five Franciscan nuns is a result of their holy living and holy dying. They lived as nuns, and died as martyrs, persecuted on land and drowned at sea. They were drowned between midnight and morning: the midnight of despair gives way to the morning of heaven, and after the terrible storm they have come to a blessed calm. The 'Lord of living and dead' (stanza 1) is their God now as he was when they were alive, for they are now with Him upon another shore and in a greater light. The poet contrasts their state with his own, in both storm and calm. While they were struggling in the storm, he was asleep in bed:

> *Away in the loveable west,*
> *On a pastoral forehead of Wales,*
> *I was under a roof here, I was at rest,*
> *And they the prey of the gales;*
> stanza 24

Now they are at peace, while the poet remains on earth with all the instability and stress which that involves:

> *I am soft sift*
> *In an hourglass – at the wall*
> *Fast, but mined with a motion, a drift,*
> *And it crowds and it combs to the fall;*
> stanza 4

This comes from the first part of the poem (stanzas 1–10), which surprises the reader who, on reading the title, expects a poem about a shipwreck. But Hopkins insisted that 'The Wreck of the Deutschland' was an ode and not primarily a narrative (L B 49), although he wrote the twelfth stanza, which begins the narrative, first (L B 44). The first part, therefore, is the opening movement of an ode. Its subject is God, as He is perceived in the human soul:

> *Thou mastering me*
> *God! giver of breath and bread;*
> *World's strand, sway of the sea;*
> *Lord of living and dead;*

Here God is 'giver of breath and bread', that is, Creator and Preserver. 'Breath' recalls the first acts of Creation in which (Genesis 2:7) 'the Lord God formed man of the dust of the ground, and breathed into his nostrils the breath of life; and man became a living soul.' 'Bread' is a reminder of the Lord's Prayer (St Matthew 6:11): 'Give us this day our daily bread.' This God, who is Creator and Preserver, is also the God who holds together the world, 'World's strand': He is the strand, or rope, of the world; or He is the strand, or shore, of the world, as if it had an edge and was totally enclosed by a seashore which is God. The contrary images jostle for space in this verse: God is 'sway of the sea', the movement to and fro of the waves, yet He is also the 'sway of the sea' in that He holds sway over it. He is both above and within the world, master of the sea, yet also the sea itself.

This God in whom all things live and move and have their being (Acts 17:28) is also the God who (each persons feels) created him and watched over him:

> *Thou hast bound bones and veins in me, fastened me flesh,*
> *And after it almost unmade, what with dread,*
> *Thy doing: and dost thou touch me afresh?*
> *Over again I feel thy finger and find thee.*

This is an astonishing imaginative perception of God, binding and fastening flesh, bones and blood together: He seems like a maker in the most simple sense, assembling the different parts. Then comes the shock

> *And after it almost unmade ...*

The fear of God, according to the poet, has almost destroyed him: it is as if the Creator had started to take him to pieces, so powerful is the sense of stress and strain conveyed by the physical imagery. This is briefly interrupted by the image of God touching the poet with His finger 'afresh', as if giving him new life (as in the Michelangelo picture of the creation of Adam in the Sistine Chapel); the images of physical strain reappear almost immediately in stanza 2:

> *I did say yes*
> *O at lightning and lashed rod;*
> *Thou heardst me truer than tongue confess*
> *Thy terror, O Christ, O God;*
> *Thou knowest the walls, altar and hour and night:*

As Peter Milward points out (*Commentary*, p. 21), the first verse had opened with 'Thou' and the second now turns to 'I'. The saying 'Yes' to God is an important feature of Hopkins' thinking. It is one function of the created self, the need to say 'Yes' to the Creator, agreeing and cooperating with Him. But the striking thing is that this is an agreement, not with a benevolent and benign Creator but with a terrifying one: this is the God and Christ of terror, the God of power and punishment, the

Christ of the lashed rod (as when he drove out the money changers from the temple). When the poet says 'Yes' to this God, he is embracing the difficulty and pain of the demands of his relationship with God. It is a private agony, as the second half of the verse suggests, with its reference to 'the walls, altar and hour and night', giving an image of a soul undergoing its own particular crisis, powerfully expressed in the images of bodily tension:

> . . . *the midriff astrain with leaning of, laced with fire of stress.*

God is now using His foot to tread upon the human soul, mastering it and almost crushing it, from such a height that it is an almost unimaginable horror:

> *The swoon of a heart that the sweep and the hurl of thee trod*
> *Hard down with a horror of height:*

These terrific ideas are conveyed by such physical images, setting up a vivid sense of discomfort and strain which corresponds to the mental and spiritual condition which we can only imagine. Saying 'Yes' is to invite such struggle and pain, but paradoxically, the same God who is so terrible is also the God who is a refuge; and only by experiencing the pain does the soul fully appreciate the sanctuary, as it flies 'with a fling of the heart to the heart of the Host' (stanza 3). From heart to heart: this is one of the three repetitions in stanza 3, the other two coming in the final line:

> *To flash from the flame to the flame then, tower from the grace to the*
> *grace.*

The poet passes from the flame, the lightning of God's purging punishment into the flame of the Holy Spirit, from the grace of fear to the grace of love. The heart in this process is 'dovewinged', in other words, inspired by the celestial dove of the Holy Spirit (which is imaged both as flame and as dove), and 'Carrier-witted', that is, given like a carrier-pigeon an instinct to make for home.

From these images of the moving soul in relation to God, punished by Him and received by Him, the poet turns back in stanza 4 to his life on earth (the first four verses alternate, God–Man–God–Man, in their openings). Now he feels the instability of his earthly life, 'soft sift / In an hourglass'; the image is again powerful, not a reflecting on the transience of life but a feeling of it. The first four lines of stanza 4 are full of such shifting movement, only to be followed by an image of stillness, of water in a well: this water is supplied by streams (which come down like ropes or veins) from the mountain, the voel (a Welsh word for a bare hill). These streams are Christ's gift of grace; and so the poem turns to a celebration of God's beauty as it is found in His gifts of creation. In stanza 5 God, or Christ, is 'under the world's splendour and wonder', underneath the surface of beautiful things, here the stars, and the dappled sky at sunset (stars, and 'dappled things' are found often in Hopkins' work). The poet kisses his hand to the Creation, to the stars and the sunset, which are evidence of the mystery of God as Creator and Redeemer:

His mystery must be instressed, stressed;
For I greet him the days I meet him, and bless when I understand.

The last line is wonderfully relaxed, with its jaunty internal rhyme ('greet him/meet him', which echoes 'under/wonder' two lines earlier) and the lovely simplicity of the ending. It is part of the changing moods of the verse in this first part of the poem. Here, however, the words 'when I understand' look back to 'mystery', suggesting that such understanding is only partial or fitful.

This moment at the end of stanza 5 is pivotal in Part I. It looks back to the earlier verses, with their description of God in mastery or majesty, revealed in terror and love. Now the verses turn from experience towards reflection and prayer; but God is at the centre of both experiences. It is His *mystery* which must be instressed and stressed. By using the word 'mystery' Hopkins is choosing a word that is a complex signifier: it can be concerned with something which is mysterious, or not clear, beyond mortal understanding. It can also mean a 'mystery' in the sense of an exclusive craft or act, something practised only by those who have special and mysterious skills (as God's creation of the natural world is an exercise of His mysterious craft). Thirdly the word 'mystery' is derived from a Greek word meaning holy, mysterious in the sense that it is not for the profane or ordinary. Each of these meanings can be supported by Christian teaching and Biblical text: in the poem they are instressed, stressed, that is they are perceived (instressed) and emphasized (stressed). Hopkins is thinking, obviously, of 'instress', of that quality which is the 'stress of being' behind inscape, behind the thisness of things: and if the world's splendour and wonder is its own gigantic inscape, the 'thisness' of the whole creation, then behind it the force and energy which sustains it is its instress, the mystery of God, which is 'stressed in' to the world, and perceived by the true eye of the believer, the yes-sayer.

If the first stanza deals with God, and the soul is dove-winged like the Holy Spirit, stanzas 6 to 8 deal with Christ the Redeemer, God Incarnate.

63

Hearts are melted (stanza 6) not by heaven but by an earthly event, a Christ whose action 'rides time like riding a river'. The image of time or life as a river is a common one, but here the idea of Christ as riding on it, from mouth to source, is transforming (it also reflects his power, as when he walked on the water, St Matthew 14:25): his life is briefly summarized in stanza 7: his time in the womb of the Virgin Mary (a warm grave for a God), his birth in the stable ('Manger', 'maiden's knee'), and then the whole life gathering to a head (Hopkins uses the grotesque and powerful image of a carbuncle or boil in the Passion, the sufferings of Christ on the cross). Since God, in Christ, rides time like a river, his presence on earth is permanent, ever-present ('Though felt before, though in high flood yet') but unacknowledged except when the heart has to do so in some crisis. It is then that decisions have to be made, for Christ or against him, to 'lash with the best or worst / Word last'. In the same way that a sloe-berry, when squeezed in the mouth, will either seem sweet (if it is ripe) or sour (if it is unripe), so the life of man will either be good or bad: but at the end all will come to the foot of the cross, 'To hero of Calvary, Christ's feet'.

Hopkins is using the *Spiritual Exercises* of St Ignatius throughout this first part. In obedience to their discipline and impulse, the first part of the poem ends (stanzas 9 and 10) with adoration of the Holy Trinity. The poet prays for the conversion of mankind ('Wring thy rebel, dogged in den / Man's malice, with wrecking and storm') and acknowledges his own contrary experience:

> *Thou art lightning and love, I found it, a winter and warm;*

the lightning and the winter are the properties of God, just as much as love and warmth: they can be used by Him to destroy man's malice with wrecking: and the image of God as 'wrecking', is, of course, crucial for the whole poem. Part I establishes that God's apparent cruelty is part of His terrifying and awe-inspiring nature: the poet himself had experienced it, but through it found true warmth and love. Now, in the description of the shipwreck that follows, there is a literal example of what has (up to now) been an image of God's behaviour, His power and His love. Hopkins is tackling the problem of evil head-on: if the question is asked 'Why did a loving God allow the *Deutschland* to be shipwrecked, and the nuns drowned?', his answer is that God's ways are beyond all understanding but that His most terrifying moments lead to His warmest and most loving ones. God as Creator and Redeemer is to be adored in His mastery and mercy, and mankind are to be brought to Him, either at once (with St Paul, stanza 10) or slowly (as St Augustine). The end of it is to make us adore Him:

Make mercy in all of us, out of us all
Mastery, but be adored, but be adored King.

The final line returns to the first four words, although now the movement is not from God to a single individual, but from God to mankind; and the first part closes with a vision of God, Father, Son and Holy Spirit, as King, King of Creation and adored by all the created world.

The first part of 'The Wreck of the Deutschland' is tense with oppositions, changes of mood and with fear of God; images that carry violently the terror and the love of God. It concentrates on the religious experience of an individual, and the possibility of religious experience for mankind; in so doing it provides a pattern and meaning for the shipwreck, by seeing it as akin to the sufferings of the truly religious man. Religion, for Hopkins, is painful, terrifying, often involving something rather like a shipwreck (the pain caused to himself and his parents by his conversion to Roman Catholicism, for example): an easy belief is not worth having ('The fear of the Lord is the beginning of wisdom', Psalm 111:10). He told Bridges that 'the poem is all strictly and literally true and did all occur; nothing is added for poetical padding' (LB 47). The first part of the poem records Hopkins' private experience of a crisis: it records, too, his ultimate acknowledgment of the mystery of God, his adoration of His mastery and mercy, and his vision of a converted world. All these are relevant to the second part.

The second part begins in stanza 11 not with God, nor with the narrative, but with the dramatic figure of Death, whose fame is set forth by drum and bugle. Some people find death by the sword, others by being run over by a train ('The flange and the rail'), others by fire, or poisonous snakes or drowning. Meanwhile we dream that we are rooted in earth, steady like a tree, only to find that we are dust. We see others die, but, waving through our short summer like the meadow-grass, we forget that the scythe will come, and the ploughshare after it. The 'sour scythe' must 'cringe', an odd word, though powerful-sounding (its old meaning was 'to fall', and in another obsolete sense it meant 'cause to cringe': either would do here, to indicate the human self at the moment of death). Hopkins is using traditional ideas ('All flesh is grass', Isaiah 40:6), but characteristically stiffening the meaning with unusual words and unaccustomed syntax.

From this strange and primitive stanza on death, Hopkins turns in stanza 12 to the narrative part of his poem, with a line that is startling in its simplicity and straightforwardness: 'On Saturday sailed from Bremen'. This is fact: the poet seems determined to respect it, and to write as unaffectedly as possible in this line. It throws into relief the preceding strain and stress, the violence of emotion, and it provides a much-needed pause in the poem before the physical violence takes over. There were, we are told, two hundred on board, including emigrants and crew, 'in the round' (approximately). They sailed (and here Hopkins cries out 'O Father') without any idea that they were going to be wrecked on a sandbank ('The goal was a shoal') or that a quarter of them would be drowned. Yet, he says, were they too not protected by the ultimate blessing and mercy of God? It is a question implying the answer: yes; that even although they perished at sea, the dark side (the side that is difficult to see into) of God's blessing (like a bay – a space between two pillars) or vault covered them: or (changing the metaphor) God's mercy acted like a rope coiled in millions of rounds, as though it could be flung out to them for ever and ever to 'reeve even them in' (to catch them, fasten them as by a reef knot).

The ship puts out to sea, in a gale and a snowstorm, leaving Bremerhaven, the safe port, behind. The language of this stanza is astonishingly accurate, with its description of the wind from east–northeast (a hated point of the compass because of the storms which usually came from there), which makes a 'regular blow' (as if a seaman were speaking), whipping up the sea into black-backed flint-flakes, and driving the snowflakes before it until they spin into the sea itself. Because of the wind the ship drifted ('drove') to leeward, and struck a sandbank so hard that

... *she beat the bank down with her bows and the ride of her keel:*

The force of the shipwreck is aptly conveyed by the rhyme-words rock / knock / shock, combined with the 'B's of 'beat the bank down' and 'breakers rolled on her beam'. Alliteration comes into its own here: the phrases come rolling over the reader like the breakers across the sandbank, which then washed over the ship: the sails were useless, the propeller ('the whorl') broken, and the wheel therefore idle.

Throughout this section of the poem, Hopkins is drawing on the newspaper reports, and the next stanza (15), 'Hope had grown grey hairs' refers to the fact that the ship lay stuck on the sandbank throughout the Monday (having struck it at about 5 a.m.) with some chance of the passengers being rescued. But passing ships did not attend to the signals: and thus the coming of the early December night, twelve hours later, was 'frightful a nightfall'. The tide was rising, so the passengers climbed into the rigging to avoid being washed away, and shook with cold and with the blowing of the wind. To make the moment more vivid, Hopkins takes a single incident, reported in *The Times* as follows:

One brave sailor, who was safe in the rigging, went down to try and save a child or woman who was drowning on deck. He was secured by a rope to the rigging, but a wave dashed him against the bulwarks, and when daylight dawned his headless body, detained by the rope, was swaying to and fro with the waves.

Hopkins' treatment is characteristic of his method. He takes from this paragraph the words that he needs, and omits those that he does not ('One' instead of 'One brave sailor', for example). He preserves enough to give the narrative credence, but then adds to it words and phrases which intensify the scene, which give the inscape, such as 'the wild woman-kind below', which suggests the distorted faces of women looking up in their agony. The man is 'handy and brave', 'handy' suggesting a man who is good with his hands; he is 'pitched to his death at a blow', thrown down in one sudden overwhelming blow of the sea, in spite of his great strength, 'his dreadnought breast and braids of thew'. The last phrases brilliantly suggest the man's chest and muscles, now thrown backwards and forwards across the deck. As they do so they form 'the burl of the fountains of air', bubbling up into the air which is itself turned to water, while the waves themselves 'buck' (like a horse) and hurl.

As the night roars on, the survivors fight with God's cold: it is God's cold, just as God is in the storm, as He was in Hopkins' own inner tempest described in Part I (it is no good being namby-pamby about God and seeking to see Him only in nice things). Hopkins faces the theological problems fairly and squarely, without any attempt to avoid the unpleasant. But God's purposes are beyond man's understanding, and it is significant that at this point in stanza 17 Hopkins introduces a heroine. This is the tall nun, who is described as 'breasting the babble' (as a breast-stroke swimmer rises above the water): she is a 'lioness' (full of courage), a 'prophetess' (filled with the divine vision) and 'a virginal tongue told' (the voice of a virgin, tolling out like a bell).

The next stanza (18) refers to the poet's own heart:

> *Ah, touched in your bower of bone,*
> *Are you!*

His heart in its bower of bone is linked with the nun 'breasting the babble': both have hearts, hers that is strong, his that is deep in feeling, and the shared emotion through the human heart is a major feature of the poem at this point. As his heart turns towards the shipwreck and the tall nun, it receives 'an exquisite smart', and words, the words of the poem 'break from me here all alone'. He is alone, writing the poem, in contrast to the tall nun, surrounded by the desperate, crying passengers. And although his heart is naturally inclined towards evil, it nevertheless utters truth in such moments of deep sympathy and feeling, and the poet's tears are evidence of the heart's possible goodness, a certain happiness even in the contemplation of such sorrow. The poet's ability to encompass such contrary impressions is remarkable here: the heart feels, utters, weeps and rejoices (from a madrigal start to a 'Never-eldering revel', a joy that never grows old). The matter for rejoicing is found in stanza 19:

> *Sister, a sister calling*
> *A master, her master and mine! –*

The lines look back to the first words of the poem: as the poet called to God then, so the sister called to Christ in her extremity of suffering. The reader hears the call, but its sound disappears beneath the 'swirling and hawling' of the inboard seas. The seas, dashing over the deck, are swirling about and hawling (hauling, but also perhaps howling), and the brine is 'sloggering', from slogger – a hard hitter is 'slogging' or hitting but also perhaps 'slobbering'. Its effect in the line

> *The rash smart sloggering brine*

is extremely powerful: the salt spray is rash, or impetuous, and smart (stinging), and also buffets the nun and blinds her: her response in that weather is to see one thing only, her vision of Christ. She lifts herself up ('rears herself to divine / Ears') and calls so that her voice is heard by the men hanging in the rigging, a meaningful sound above the storm's brawling.

We learn in the next stanza (20) that she was the chief sister in the group of five German nuns: Hopkins then reflects on the circumstances which brought about their presence on the ship. Not only was the ship called the *Deutschland*, but the country was Deutschland also ('double a desperate name') birthplace of Luther and of the anti-Catholic Falck laws. Luther and St Gertrude, the German mystic and Roman Catholic saint, were both from Eisleben, and Hopkins sees this as an emblem of the way in which good and evil exist inseparably in the world (Abel is Cain's brother . . .). The foolish description of Luther as a 'beast of the waste wood' (following the words of a sixteenth-century Pope) is a blemish on the poem which has to be accepted as a natural part of

Hopkins' intense Roman Catholicism: here he sees the death of the nun as an example of the evil in a fallen world ('O world wide of its good!') and that evil is evidenced in Cain and Luther. Hopkins ignores Luther's greatness partly because he sees him as part of the long historical process which led to the exile of the nuns from Germany. They are 'Banned by the land of their birth' (stanza 21), and 'Loathed for a love men knew in them', that is hated (as Christ said his disciples would be) for their love of God. Thrown out by one river (the Rhine) they were shipwrecked at the mouth of another (the Thames), attacked, as if by a monster gnashing its teeth (which looks forward to 'endragonèd seas', stanza 27). Again, the traditional image of evil as a dragon is evoked as the sea rages:

> *Surf, snow, river and earth*
> *Gnashed:*

But above and beyond such powers of evil is the figure of Christ, the great hunter of wickedness ('Orion of light'). He is the 'martyr-master' also, that is the master of martyrs (the nuns) but also the master who has been a martyr, whose

> *. . . unchancelling poising palms were weighing the worth,*

unchancelling (a word invented by Hopkins) probably means 'leaving nothing to chance': so Christ, who weighs all things in his poised hands, turns evil to good, seeing flowers in the snowflakes, lilies in heaven now found on the white earth.

The poem is moving swiftly from the terrible and violent description of the wreck, to a vision of the whole scene through eyes that are trained to interpret such scenes with all the apparatus of Roman Catholic liturgy and symbolism. So the five nuns become important because they are five, corresponding in number to the five wounds of Christ. Five is the 'finding' (the means by which we find and count), the 'sake' (the 'essence' – as in 'namesake', 'keepsake'), and the 'cipher' (the code, which we interpret to find the truth). These wounds (marks) are made by mankind: Hopkins urges us (switching from verb to noun) to 'Mark, the mark . . .': the marks are man-made, and the word which man uses for it is 'Sacrificed' ('Christ our passover is sacrificed for us'). But it is God who allows such sacrifice or martyrdom:

> *But he scores it in scarlet himself on his own bespoken,*
> *Before time-taken, dearest prizèd and priced –*

Those (like Christ, and the nuns) who are taken 'before their time' are marked by God (scored with scarlet, the colour of Christ's blood), with the sign (stigma, signal) of the five wounds which become the five leaves ('cinquefoil token') of the mystic rose. Hopkins sees the rose mark as lettering on the fleece of the lamb (Christ the sacrificial lamb) and the redness on the rose-flake comes from the blood of Christ too, since Christ is all in all by his sacrifice.

After this concentrated and difficult verse, the poem turns to St Francis: his reception of the stigmata ('the gnarls of the nails in thee, niche of the lance') was a seal of his sainthood; for the nuns, too, the seal is the wild waters, where they bathe in the mercy of God. In their suffering, therefore, they are exalted: by contrast the poet (stanza 24) remembers that he was safely in bed while all this was going on. While he was asleep under a roof, the tall nun was calling 'O Christ, Christ, come quickly'; in so doing she was transforming her sorrow into joy, turning her cross into Christ, *christening* the destruction by her shouting of the word.

The next stanza (25) begins with the words 'The majesty!' They refer to what Hopkins sees as the majestic figure of the nun, transforming the elements with the courage of a lioness. He then prays twice

> *Breathe, arch and original Breath . . .*
> *Breathe, body of lovely Death . . .*

Both are prayers for inspiration ('breathing in') the first from God the creator, the second from Christ who died. The question in the first line, 'what did she mean?' is taken up by other questions later in the verse: did she call Christ to her for love of him (as if he had been her lover), or was she consciously seeking a martyr's crown? Either way she is contrasted with the disciples who were frightened in the storm on the sea of Galilee, who woke Jesus, saying, 'Lord save us: we perish' (St Matthew 8:25).

Her majestic bearing and her aspiration towards Christ are cheering to the poet. Just as the nun will feel the comfort of heaven more powerfully after enduring the sufferings of earth, so the poet feels the coming of spring after winter (stanza 26), and beyond that, the heaven which 'eye hath not seen nor ear heard':

The treasure never eyesight got, nor was ever guessed what for the hearing?

This may have been a motive for the nun's behaviour, and it is a continuation of the meditation, so that stanzas 25 and 26 belong together. In the five stanzas which follow, Hopkins takes the argument a stage further, into the heart of the poem's religious significance. The difficult stanza 27 argues that it is not the love of Christ, nor danger, 'electrical horror' which 'fathers' (the crucial verb) such a state of mind. Another motive lies behind it, something more powerful than any of these: it is the sense of the presence of God Himself –

> *the Master,*
> Ipse, *the only one, Christ, King, Head:*

The early part of this stanza (28) prepares the reader for the expression of the inexpressible. It is almost as if the figure itself looms out of the darkness of our perception, caught by the nun in her moment of transfiguration and ecstasy. The impact of the accumulated nouns – 'the Master, *Ipse*, the only one, Christ, King, Head' – is as overwhelming as it is intended to be. The emphasis is once again on mastery, but it is also on the uniqueness, the *inscape* of Christ himself, he is Christ, *Ipse*, himself, the only one, who comes to save the nun in her extremity. Her readiness for this is vital: her heart is right (stanza 29) and her eye fixed; she is steady as a rock (but is also a light-house):

> *The Simon Peter of a soul! to the blast*
> *Tarpeian-fast, but a blown beacon of light.*

If she is a beacon of light, she is reflecting the light of Jesus (stanza 30), and Jesus is the son of Mary. Now, the *Deutschland* struck the sandbank on 6 December, lay there all day, and most of the deaths happened on the following night, 6–7 December. 7 December is the eve of the feast of the Immaculate Conception, which is referred to in stanza 30. But while the nun is possessed of Christ, what about the others, the unbelievers, the 'Comfortless unconfessed of them' (stanza 31)? The poet's answer is conveyed in one of his most nimble images.

> *lovely-felicitous Providence*
> *Finger of a tender of, O of a feathery delicacy, the breast of the*
> *Maiden could obey so, be a bell to, ring of it, and*
> *Startle the poor sheep back!*

The maiden is here calling the unfaithful by her cry to Christ, like a bell, or like a shepherd startling the lost sheep back into the fold: this is the providence of God, so that the shipwreck becomes a harvest, the tempest carries the grain (removes the chaff of unbelief and leaves the grain of goodness).

So the poet moves into his final four stanzas of adoration and prayer (32–5). Stanza 32 is a magnificent evocation of the power of God, the God of the sea, and of tides, and of seasons, God as the ground of all being 'and granite of it'. Not only is He the magnificent God of Creation, He is also (33) the God of mercy, Christ the redeemer; as God saved

71

Noah, so here He provides an ark of hope against the flood; and as Christ walked on the water, he is present even in the wreck

The Christ of the Father compassionate, fetched in the storm of his strides.

From the Father and the Son, Hopkins turns naturally to the Holy Spirit in stanza 34: 'Now burn' is a reference to the pentecostal fire of the spirit (Acts 2:3), although he returns almost immediately to Christ and Mary, who are miraculous in the spirit of love, 'Miracle-in-Mary-of-flame'. Christ has a 'Double-naturèd name' because he is the son of God and the son of Mary: flung from heaven, having a heart of flesh, and furled within the womb of the Virgin Mary.

But God, Father, Son and Holy Spirit, the three of the thunder-throne, are so magnificent that we need intercession. In common with Roman Catholic practice, Hopkins prays to the tall nun (the 'Dame, at our door / Drowned') to ask her to intercede for England and the English: she was drowned at the mouth of the Thames, and now is the bringing back of Christ to England (absent, in Hopkins' eyes, since the Reformation). Christ in England would be like a new resurrection ('Let him easter in us') and a light in our darkness, a dayspring and a new dawn. So Britain will become brighter ('More brightening her') as the reign of Christ begins: since the poem began with 'Thou mastering me / God', it appropriately ends with God as the fire of our charity and Lord of our best thoughts.

5. The Spring Poems of 1877

The poems written in north Wales during the spring of 1877 are among Hopkins' finest, and certainly his most accessible and buoyant. The poems which he wrote during this period were:

God's Grandeur
The Starlight Night (sent to his mother in a letter postmarked March 3)
Spring (May 1877)
The Lantern out of Doors
The Sea and the Skylark (Rhyl, May 1877)
The Windhover (St Beuno's, May 1877)

These short poems, more than any other of Hopkins' work, are concerned with the praise of God the Creator. In the Commentary on the *Spiritual Exercises*, he begins 'The First Principle and Foundation' with the words: 'Man was created to praise, reverence and serve God Our Lord, and by so doing to save his soul.' (SD 122) God is 'deeply present to everything' (SD 128), and a further note adds:

God's utterance of himself is God the Word, outside himself is this world. This world then is word, expression, news of God. Therefore its end, its purpose, its purport, its meaning, is God and its life or work to name and praise him. (SD 129)

It follows that to neglect the beauty of the world is to ignore God: to write poems that glorify Him is a joyful duty for a priest, when other duties (imposed by the vows of obedience) permit. The underlying impulse behind these poems is therefore religious.

'God's Grandeur'

The world is charged with the grandeur of God.

As a first line this is uncompromising. Its rhythm is confident and assured, and the full stop at the end of the line seems to emphasize the completeness and finality of the statement. The world is charged with God's grandeur, and that is that. Hopkins was so careful with line-endings and rhythms that this sentence within a line is evidently there for a purpose, to make the claim as strongly as possible. It does so especially because of the emphatic word 'charged', which usefully has two meanings: 'loaded', and 'full of electricity' as a battery is when it has been charged. The world is therefore electric with God's grandeur, and loaded with it (which suggests that the grandeur is heavy and substantial): the image of electricity is carried on in the second line, when he senses that the grandeur of God will 'flame out, like shining from shook foil'. As foil, when shaken, gives off shining light, so the world, when looked at carefully, is full of the shining light of God Himself, leaping out like flames or sparks. Hopkins described it to Bridges as 'I mean foil in its sense of leaf or tinsel, . . . Shaken gold foil gives off broad glares like sheet lightning, and this is true of nothing else, owing to its zigzag dints and creasings and network of small many cornered facets, a sort of fork lightning too.' (LB 169) Its fullness is indicated by the next image

> *It gathers to a greatness, like the ooze of oil*
> *Crushed.*

Hopkins is here thinking of an olive press, with the oil oozing from the pressed fruit. It oozes from every part of the press, in a fine film, and then the trickles gather together to form a jar of oil. In the same way the grandeur of God is found everywhere, trickling from every simple thing in the created universe and accumulating to form a greatness, a grandeur that is perceived by the discerning mind of the Christian and poet. This is made clear in the lines which follow, which are a lament for the neglect and indifference shown by mankind. Once again the poetry is dense with metaphors: instead of saying 'why do men take no notice?' Hopkins writes

> *Why do men then now not reck his rod?*

The rhythms and sounds are themselves awkward, like the question: 'men then', 'now not' and 'reck his rod' (care for his rule: 'reck' means 'heed', occurring in ordinary speech in the word 'reckless'). And these sounds continue, as if Hopkins is using the vocabulary and rhythms of his verse to act out, as well as describe, the situation:

> *Generations have trod, have trod, have trod;*
> > *And all is seared with trade; bleared, smeared with toil;*
> > *And wears man's smudge and shares man's smell: the soil*
> *Is bare now, nor can foot feel, being shod.*

Here the mechanical forces are captured in verse by the heavy accents.

What is sometimes called the 'daily grind' is a repetitive thump in which the feet of generations march on; and the 'trod . . . trod . . . trod' sets up the three-beat rhythm of the next line: 'seared . . . bleared . . . smeared'. The verbs themselves sprawl across the line, preventing any delicacy of feeling or perception. 'Seared', for instance, means 'dried up' or it can mean 'rendered incapable of feeling': it is accompanied by 'bleared' (blurred with inflammation of the eyes) and 'smeared' (rubbed over with dirt). When we think of the minute attention to detail of Hopkins' drawings, these adjectives take on yet more force: they are part of the process of treading down, smudging and generally spoiling, nature. Because of this the soil is barren, and feet, being shod with boots, cannot feel it. For Hopkins the 'foot feel' is but a part of the whole process of insensitivity: as a man's feet are encased in boots, so his whole soul is bound up, unfree.

The process of the octave of this sonnet is a very interesting one, involving as it does a number of images which spread their meanings in many directions. The richness of the similes and metaphors is over-whelming: they create a very powerful sense of beauty and greatness that is being systematically neglected and crushed. (It is for this reason that Hopkins writes in 'Inversnaid' of the 'wildness and wet', the need to leave nature alone. It is a commonplace idea now, in an age of National Parks and wilderness areas, but in Hopkins' day it was fresh and original).

It is then that the sestet throws into the equation another mysterious force, the unending freshness and growth of nature that causes it to live on, to survive against all the neglect and exploitation of man. Its nature is in this way to be itself: to go on growing each year with its own processes of generation and renewed life, so that against the unfeeling energies of man there is placed something greater, the inexhaustible forces of nature. Its spirit of growth is everywhere: it is as natural and inevitable as the coming of morning after nightfall. It is the 'dearest freshness' deep down in things which ensures that 'nature is never spent'; and in the final lines this inexhaustible quality is associated with the working of the Holy Ghost, the spirit of God who created all things and sustains them:

> *Because the Holy Ghost over the bent*
> *World broods with warm breast and with ah! bright wings.*

'The Starlight Night'

'The Starlight Night' is a different kind of linguistic exercise. It is characteristic of Hopkins that he should have entitled the poem 'Starlight Night'
and not 'Starlit Night': the assonance light/night is a foretaste of the
pleasing shocks and surprises that are to follow. The first two lines, for
example, move astonishingly from the colloquial and dramatic:

> *Look at the stars! look, look up at the skies!*

which might be spoken by anyone, especially (like a child) in a state of
excitement; to the imaginative

> *O look at all the fire-folk sitting in the air!*

Each star becomes a fire-person, and together they are the fire-folk,
living in their towns and cities:

> *The bright boroughs, the circle-citadels there!*

They have their own landscape, with woods and diamond mines
('delves'); they shine like the eyes of elves, and have lawns shining with
'quickgold' (a word formed by analogy with 'quicksilver'). The excited
imagination peoples the heavens with a whole society: it leaps exultingly
from feature to feature, exclaiming (the exclamation-marks are important in this respect). The stars are like trees, moving in the wind or
lighted by the sun, small trees (whitebeam) and white poplars ('abeles set
on a flare'); or like doves, fluttering in a farmyard when they are scared
by something. These images are extraordinarily remote from the objects
themselves, the stars in the sky: and yet in trying to compare them, the
reader's sensibility makes its own imaginative effort, and becomes as
excited as the poet's. The difficulty is in bringing the mind back from
such voyages of discovery among the stars: and Hopkins manages this
with supreme skill:

> *Ah well! it is all a purchase, all is a prize.*

The 'Ah well!' seems to look back to all the other exclamations, and then
to be an exclamation of a different kind, a moment of reflection and a
pause after the headlong rush of imagery. It is a good example of Hopkins' ability to rejuvenate old phraseology: 'Ah well!' is most frequently
a phrase with a tinge of regret in it, but here it seems to be just a
transitional moment from exclamation and excitement to reflection.
When the poet reflects that 'it is all a purchase, all is a prize', he seems to
be thinking that the starlit sky is abundant, like a market stall or a

fairground booth set out with a great variety of things. Yet it might also be said that it is a 'purchase', something which can give a grip on to something, and a 'prize' in the sense that it is a reward for the onlooker with the right spirit and the true mind. It is he who can buy or make offers for this purchase or prize. He is able to take all this richness into himself, to possess it, if he has the correct wherewithal:

> *Buy then! bid then! – What? – Prayer, patience, alms, vows.*

The purchase of prize comes to the person who prays, has patience, gives freely and dedicates himself. When he has done so, he again sees the fresh excitement of the stars, like spring blossom on orchards or the yellow gleam on willow-catkins:

> *Look, look: a May-mess, like on orchard boughs!*
> *Look! March-bloom, like on mealed-with-yellow sallows!*

The last three lines of the sestet are perhaps the most difficult:

> *These are indeed the barn; withindoors house*
> *The shocks. The piece-bright paling shuts the spouse*
> *Christ home, Christ and his mother and all his hallows.*

Hopkins is here thinking of gathered corn (the 'shocks' or stooks of corn): if the stars are the barn, then what is inside the barn is infinitely more precious. The brilliant stars (the piece-bright paling) are a wall or paling that encloses Christ who is the 'spouse', the husband and father of all this beauty: the paling 'shuts Christ home', as a man is shut in when he comes home from work at the end of a day. With him is his mother, the blessed Virgin Mary, and all his saints (hallows). The stars are what the eye can perceive, and yet embodied in them is the power of God Incarnate, of the holy ones who have actually been made known to mankind. So the sonnet which begins with 'Look', ends with 'hallows', with the stars as saints in light.

A poem such as this may be seen as the instinctive reaction of an imaginative person to the sparkling beauty of the night sky: but in Hopkins' individual view the stars have become compared with fairy things, trees, farmyard doves; all things that enable him to see them more clearly with his mind. Only then, when the inscape has been established (or rather, the *more* the inscape is established) does the true sense of God's presence become known. The more fully a beautiful thing is seen and felt, the more the nature of God is revealed.

'Spring'

The same division into octave and sestet, description and reflection, is found in 'Spring', though not so fancifully. As so often the first line is simple, arresting, uncompromising, utterly unaffected:

> *Nothing is so beautiful as Spring –*

and it is followed by a line that is very characteristic of Hopkins in its idiosyncracy:

> *When weeds, in wheels, shoot long and lovely and lush;*

weeds are not usually thought of as being like wheels, yet the comparison perfectly suggests the roundness of grass weeds. They are usually regarded, too, as a nuisance; and it is like Hopkins (who loved wildness in all forms) to admire them for themselves, as examples of the fertile and creative impulse of spring. And as he compared the stars with trees and shining lawns in 'The Starlight Night', so now he compares birds' eggs with the sky:

> *Thrush's eggs look little low heavens ...*

The image, as so often in Hopkins, is a freshening of the old and traditional. Here he might have said 'Thrush's eggs are sky-blue', but he prefers to see them in terms of the sky-heaven itself, but a little, low, heaven. And when the thrush sings, it seems to take the ear and clean it, as if the ear had been washed

> *and thrush*
> *Though the echoing timber does so rinse and wring*
> *The ear, it strikes like lightnings to hear him sing;*

'the echoing timber' for woodland is not one of Hopkins' more successful images, for it gives the suggestion of dead wood; but the sound and sense of 'rinse and wring' suggest the piercing physical washing and turning of the ear, so that the freshness of sound strikes like lightnings. Everywhere in this poem it is this new freshness which is emphasized: the shiny leaves of the pear tree ('The glassy peartree leaves and blooms'), seen against the sky seem to 'brush / The descending blue', as though green against blue is newly painted and the blue heaven is getting nearer and nearer. Blue is the colour of this octave, counterpointed with green, the green of the weeds and the pear trees: against the background of blue there is green, and against the background of green there are the racing lambs.

The technique of this kind of verse is to use colour, sound and movement to create an impression of a vibrating and rich natural world, a world free of 'juice and . . . joy' as the first line of the sestet has it. It is, we are told, a 'strain' or remote descendant of paradise:

> *A strain of the earth's sweet being in the beginning*
> *In Eden garden.*

The poem then twists into a prayer for young people, for those who are in the 'springtime' of life, before their lives have been cloyed, clouded or soured. Christ, who was himself young ('maid's child'), is asked to preserve 'Innocent mind and Mayday in girl and boy'. Hopkins' love of all things fresh, youthful, promising is well recorded here: it is part of a certain quality of innocence in his verse which is extremely attractive and which is allied to his perception of human and natural beauty.

'The Lantern out of Doors'

Colours were very important to Hopkins, as his notebooks and poems suggest; at Kew in May 1874 he noticed the Old Palace – 'ruddled red brick over a close-shaven green-white lawn; chestnuts in bloom and a beech in a fairy spray of green' (JP 243) – and on the Isle of Man (August 1873) he noted:

Painted white cobbled foam tumbling over the rocks and combed away off their sides again. The water-ivybush, that plucked and dapper cobweb of glassy grey down, swung slack and jaunty on the in-shore water, plainer where there was dark weed below and dimmer over bare rock or sand. On the cliffs fields of bleached grass, the same colour as the sheep they feed, then a sleeve of liquid barleyfield, then another slip of bleached grass, above that fleshy blue sky. (JP 235)

Both in his appreciation of colours and in his sense of light and dark, Hopkins was fundamentally and powerfully aware of contrast. This is found in 'The Lantern out of Doors', where the light of lanterns in the darkness is likened to good men in a wicked world (as it is by Portia in *The Merchant of Venice*, which may have been in Hopkins' mind as he thought of countrymen with lanterns). In one of his sermons, on the first Sunday in Advent (1879), Hopkins preaches on light and darkness, seeing our life as night and Christ's coming as the day. He showed himself to be fascinated by the contrasts and changes of night and day:

79

to most men the daylight is the place to work in but those that work in the pit go where all is darker than night and work by candlelight and when they see the light of day again their work is over, as if day were night to them and night day, so then this life is dark, a pit, but we work in it; death will shew us daylight, but all our work will then be done. (SD 39)

Hopkins sees them go with a colloquial 'and out of sight is out of mind'; but in his theology 'Christ minds', that is Christ thinks about them and cares about what happens to them. The dense compression of Hopkins' language forces into the final lines a number of the attributes of Christ, who sees man, longs for him, cares for him, follows him with kindly foot, ransoms, rescues and befriends:

> *Christ minds: Christ's interest, what to avow or amend*
> *There, éyes them, heart wánts, care haúnts, foot fóllows kínd,*
> *Their ránsom, théir rescue, ánd first, fást, last friénd.*

'The Sea and the Skylark'

'The Lantern out of Doors' depends on the perception of contrast between light and dark. Similarly, 'The Sea and the Skylark' pictures the poet standing on the shore (it was written at Rhyl, in May 1877) hearing at one ear the sea, and at the other the skylark – 'two noises too old to end'. These sounds 'Trench': they *dig* into the poet's ear, in a characteristically forceful word. And because the poem is about sounds, the lines use sound and rhythm patterns to recreate the noise that the ear hears. The sea 'ramps against the shore' (the sound of waves breaking) and the lark's clipped song in the wind is heard

> *In crisps of curl off wild winch whirl, and pour*
> *And pelt music . . .*

A letter to Bridges, written in 1882, shows how much care and thought went into the portrayal of the lark's song in words:

The skein and coil are the lark's song, which from his height gives the impression (not to me only) of something falling to the earth and not vertically quite but tricklingly or wavingly, something as a skein of silk ribbed by having been tightly wound on a narrow card or notched holder or as fishingtackle or twine unwinding from a reel or winch, or as pearls strung on a horsehair: the laps or folds are the notes or short measures or bars of them . . . The lark in wild glee races the reel round, paying or dealing out and down the turns of the skin or coil right to the earth floor . . . (LB 164)

Both lark and sea are pure and natural: and in a Wordsworth-like sestet, Hopkins complains that they

> *. . . ring right out our sordid turbid time,*
> *Being pure! We, life's pride and cared-for crown,*
>
> *Have lost that cheer and charm of earth's past prime: . . .*

The complaint that nature is pure and clean and man is not is a commonplace of eighteenth- and nineteenth-century poetry, and this poem, skilful though its sound-work is, is one of Hopkins' least original sonnets. He said himself (of the lark-song image) that 'I felt even at the time that in the endless labour of recasting those lines I had lost the freshness I wanted and which indeed the subject demands.' (LB 164) That freshness was rediscovered in 'The Windhover'.

'The Windhover'

Hopkins described 'The Windhover' as 'the best thing I ever wrote' (LB 85). It dates from 30 May 1877 and is the climactic poem of the fine series written in north Wales during that creative spring. 'Windhover' is an old word for a kestrel.

Certain critics (especially anti-Christian and anti-Jesuit ones) have seen the poem as one of frustration and sadness, which is concerned with the unbridgeable distance between the hawk, flying so freely and beautifully, and the poet, whose heart is 'in hiding'; the heart is hidden away as if afraid, locked up by the severe discipline of the priesthood and the demands of self-sacrifice which it makes.

Yet the poem does not seem to be a poem of frustration so much as a poem of enthusiasm and exultation, followed by a mature and quiet consideration. It resembles 'The Starlight Night' in its octave, that excited perception of natural beauty; and its sestet (as in 'The Starlight Night') is reflective, but more gracefully and less doctrinally so. The excitement is conveyed in the way in which the heart, while it may have been 'in hiding', that is inactive, now 'Stirred for a bird'; as if the heart moved and leaped at the sight of the hawk. Hopkins is writing a poem in which, above all, he *recognizes* beauty and exults in it. In 'The Wreck of the Deutschland' he had written:

> I kiss my hand
> To the stars, lovely-asunder
> Starlight, wafting him out of it; . . .
>> stanza 5

The 'him' is Christ, revealed in starlight, or in thunder, or in 'the dappled-with-damson west', the sunset:

> *His mystery must be instressed, stressed;*
> *For I greet him the days I meet him, and bless when I understand.*

In this way 'The Windhover' is a poem of 'greeting', of meeting God, Christ, in the flight and movement of the bird; and then, at the end, reflecting on more ordinary beauties which occur in the created world. If they are so beautiful (the newly-turned earth in a furrow, the colours of a falling log in the fire) no wonder the hawk speaks to the beholder of something infinitely more marvellous.

The title of the poem is 'The Windhover': not 'The Hawk' or 'The Kestrel', but 'The Windhover': as though the poet is already describing the bird not by its usual ornithological name, but by its attributes, by what it does (in a *kenning*). What it does itself, supremely, the hoverer in the wind, the rider of the air; and so the very title takes us into the nature of the thing itself. The name of the windhover is followed by 'To Christ our Lord'; it is as if there is a relationship between the bird and Christ, one which the poem will make clear; 'The Windhover's (purpose) is to Christ our Lord' or 'The Windhover (leads us) to Christ our Lord'. Certainly the sub-title or subsidiary phrase in the title, or the dedication, whatever it may be, is important in that it points at once beyond the physical to the metaphysical: that is, it raises questions at the outset about the hawk as the representative, not of a bird-species, but of the power of God in the universe. The poet is contemplating something brilliant and wonderful, which states itself in its actions, and in so doing states God: as Hopkins writes in the Commentary on the *Spiritual Exercises*, discussing the Holy Ghost:

All things therefore are charged with love, are charged with God and if we know how to touch them give off sparks and take fire, yield drops and flow, ring and tell of him. (SD 195)

This is what is happening in 'The Windhover': the bird gives off sparks and takes fire, rings and tells of God, because the poet, through the working of the Holy Spirit, knows how to touch it. That touching is what the poem itself demonstrates: and for this reason it begins with the poet himself, 'I caught' – not I saw. or I watched, but 'I caught'. This could mean 'I caught sight of', but it also means, more powerfully, 'I caught', almost as a hunter catches a bird: I 'took' it, made it my own.

The 'I' is of course as important as the 'caught', for the poem is about an encounter between a human being and natural object. between the internal and the external world. Plenty of people might have seen the hawk and admired it (or even ignored it), but only the poet could have seen it and written about it with such intensity. So the 'I', the very first syllable of the poem, is important: it is picked up later in the 'my heart in hiding' image, which helps to remind the reader of the other force in the poem beside the hawk, the perceiving and feeling mind of the poet.

What the perceiving and feeling mind caught was the windhover itself, but the language used to describe it is astonishing even for Hopkins:

> *I caught this morning morning's minion, king-*
> *dom of daylight's dauphin, dapple-dawn-drawn Falcon . . .*

In stopping the quotation at that point, the writer becomes aware how artificial such partial quotation of Hopkins is: the sonnet is all of a piece, and its rhythms and ideas cannot be disconnected one from the other. But for the purposes of discussion, we may observe the extraordinary alliteration of m/n in the first line: 'morning morning's minion', the whole giving an impression of movement repeated. The meaning is, of course, that during the morning the poet saw the minion (darling, favourite) of the morning: but the sound suggests also a less logical reading of the line, in which the double morning suggests that it was a 'morning of mornings', in which the poet caught the 'minion/king'. 'Kingdom' is related to the phrase which follows. in which the windhover is prince (dauphin) of the kingdom of daylight: but for a split second at the end of the line he is king also, as the sounds take one meaning and then another. The introduction of 'dauphin', with all its connotations of the French court, is a piece of daring: it picks up the French origin of 'minion' (mignon) and adds its own sense of glamour, distinction, and royalty. The hawk is the favourite and the prince of the morning: only now is he described in bird terms, as a 'dapple-dawn-drawn Falcon'. The triple word is an artificially made adjective, whose 'd's link up with 'dom/daylight's/dauphin/', and postpone the arrival of the word 'Falcon'. The falcon is 'drawn' or pictured against the early morning sky, the dappled dawn: but any suggestion that it is somehow passive, or just a picture, is removed by the forceful simplicity of 'in his riding . . . and striding'. Both words are extremely important, indicating a command of the elements and in particular a powerful mastery of the air. The Falcon is seen

> *in his riding*
> *of the rolling level underneath him steady air*

which seems to mean that he is riding (as a horseman might) across the rolling level, with steady air beneath him, between him and the ground: although the syntax is beautifully uncertain and there is a suggestion that he might be riding the steady air ('the rolling level underneath him'). In this riding he is masterfully striding (walking powerfully, or perhaps *be*striding) and 'striding/High there': the two long syllables of 'High there' (a fine example of the use of sprung rhythm) are strangely effective. It is almost as if they develop into 'Hi, there!' as the poet sees the bird and greets it. But the primary sense is still of great height, as the bird controls its flight so perfectly:

> *how he rung upon the rein of a wimpling wing*
> *In his ecstasy!*

The sounds here balance and interconnect – rung . . . wing . . . wimpling . . . rein . . . / rung . . . rein . . . ring, and, again, at moments such as this it is useful to remember that Hopkins was an occasional composer of music. Vowels and consonants act in successive different but related stressed notes, until the next line provides its own quaver trill. 'In his ecstasy!' The last phrase ends with a lovely rest on the exclamation mark, before the line moves off again, just as the bird's flight pauses and moves, and as a piece of music will start again after a rest:

> *then off, off forth on swing,*
> *As a skate's heel sweeps smooth on a bow-bend: the hurl and gliding*
> *Rebuffed the big wind.*

The long line of sprung rhythm (fifteen syllables) is remarkably effective here: it carries the image of the hawk swinging round in flight in a long arc, like the arc made by the heel of an ice-skate, and then carries it one stage further. The ice-skate image cannot be seen to over-dominate the picture, or its fixedness would contrast too strongly with the free movements of the flying hawk. So the air-images are brought into play again – 'hurl', 'gliding' and the plosive-sound of 'Rebuffed the big wind'.

At this point, having described the riding and the swing of the bird in the wind, the poet returns to himself. Characteristically, the insight comes through rhyming words

> *My heart in hiding*
> *Stirred for a bird,*

The phrase 'Stirred for a bird' seems almost childish; yet here it reaches through the complicated imagery towards an important simplicity, the actual sensation of the heart moving (as we say 'my heart sank' or as Wordsworth says 'My heart leaps up when I behold/A rainbow . . .'). Here the heart is stirred by the bird, and especially by 'the achieve of, the mastery of the thing!' The 'achieve(ment)': Hopkins is using a verb as a noun to give new life and meaning, and 'the mastery of the thing!' is a summing up of the windhover's perfection, its absolute mastery of the air and wind.

The octave is a quite extraordinary mixture of sound, rhythm and visual imagery, succeeding in re-enacting the hawk's flight as the poet sees and feels it. And then the sestet, instead of turning reflective, drives the excitement yet further. Throughout the poem, the pauses and movements interact: now, after the complete pause at the end of line 8, the energy is gathered up again.

> *Brute beauty and valour and act, oh, air, pride, plume, here*
> *Buckle!*

The line begins with a near assonance, 'Brute beauty', an unusual combination both in sound and sense, but (as so often in Hopkins) one that makes his own kind of sense. The 'Brute beauty' is not 'brutal' except in the most literal sense, that it is the beauty of a creature; yet as the word 'Brute' suggests strength and even 'brutality', as in 'brute force', so it conveys the sense of the hawk's power. Brute force becomes 'Brute beauty', to be followed by the exotic French-derived word 'valour'. 'Valour' suggests bravery or courage; its Frenchness links up with 'dauphin' to give the hawk an exotic presence. This is added to 'Brute beauty' and followed by 'act' (short for 'action') to make a series of attributes added together: brute beauty plus valour plus act, followed by a pause on 'oh' and then an acceleration 'oh, air, pride, plume, here'. At this point the attributes of the hawk become disparate, yet joined: the air of which it is master, the pride it seems to have in its power, the actual feathers of which its wings are made, all come together to supplement the first three, brute beauty, valour and act(ion). By this time the reader has been confronted with no less than six nouns: the line is looking desperately for a verb to give them meaning and to place them in a sentence. What do all these things do? The answer is held back even further by the use of the word 'here' at the end of the line, which increases the sense of immediacy. Then, as we cross back to the following line, we find the word 'Buckle!' with all the force of its hard sounds and its exclamation mark.

It is a crucial word, and it is crucially placed. Its position at the beginning of the line, after such a build-up of nouns, ensures that it arrives with tremendous emphasis. That emphasis is increased by the fact that it is in the present tense. Until this moment the sonnet has been in the past tense – 'I *caught* this morning . . .' 'My heart . . . Stirred for a bird'. Now the moment is thrown into the present: it is 'here' and 'now'. The word 'here' prepares us for this: and it is as though the power and glory of the bird have broken through normal time. The remembrance of the bird has given way to the realization of the bird, as if it were now present rather than past: the bird is *here*, *now*, rather than there, then. It is given a kind of incarnation as it becomes no longer a memory but a presence, and in this process the words of dedication in the title 'To Christ our Lord' assume an important significance. They suggest that the windhover in its magnificence is a type or emblem of all glorious and masterful things, of which the greatest is Christ. They manifest, in their mastery and glory, something which is not subject to time but is somehow present, as the hawk's qualities are in itself, here and now. And as Christ is glorious, so He is found in the hawk at this moment. It is as though the hawk moves out of the ordinary world of past, present and future into a world where these things are transcended. God, in the words of Hopkins' Commentary on the *Spiritual Exercises,*

Carries the creature to or towards the end of its being, which is its selfsacrifice to God and its salvation ... all is done through Christ, Christ's spirit ... It is as if a man said: That is Christ playing at me and me playing at Christ, only that it is no play but truth; That is Christ *being me* and me being Christ. (SD 154).

The windhover at this moment is being Christ and Christ is being it, condensing within itself all the attributes of beauty, courage, action, 'air, pride, plume'. It is here that we find difficulty with the word 'Buckle!' What does it mean?

It does not help to press this question too far. The force of the word is as important as its meaning, and poems are not paraphrasable into prose summaries anyway. But the primary meaning is probably 'join together' (as in 'buckle my shoe'), suggesting that all the qualities of the previous line buckle together in the hawk. Given the other suggestions of chivalry in the poem ('valour', 'chevalier'), this may also contain the idea of buckling on armour, as though the windhover buckles on to itself all the attributes – air, pride, plume, beauty, valour, action. It could also suggest buckle in the sense of 'give way under stress', as a piece of metal folds beneath a particular force and weight. This could then be a visual image for the way in which the hawk, having held itself still and hovering in the air (as kestrels do) almost rigid except for the movement of its wings, suddenly bends and dives. Its swoop downwards is as if the shape had suddenly buckled and fallen. Or (as some critics think), it is an image of the natural order (the hawk) buckling beneath a greater, supernatural reality. All earthly things (brute beauty, valour, act and so on) buckle as the windhover dives and becomes transfigured:

> *... AND the fire that breaks from thee then, a billion*
> *Times told lovelier, more dangerous. O my chevalier!*

Here Hopkins seems to see fire breaking from the bird as it dives, a fire of energy or of a spirit. It comes at the moment when all things 'buckle' in the hawk; as though at this particular second all its beauty is held in a wonderful unity of perfection. The 'A N D', printed in capitals, promotes a normally insignificant word, 'and', into a major role. The reader has to pause, to give it emphasis, to see the word as a slow step in the line: it is the verbal equivalent of a pause before movement, of the moment of perfection (say of a diver on a diving-board, committed to a dive yet not fully into it). It is followed by the suggestion that in its movement the hawk is 'a billion/Times told lovelier, more dangerous. O my chevalier!' The 'thee' in the line before suggests that Hopkins is here addressing the bird: as with 'dauphin' and 'valour', he uses a French-derived word, now suggesting a chivalrous knight.

The traditional reflective comment is held back until the last three lines of this sonnet, making a sudden *pianissimo* after the excitement and exotic power of the previous three lines. Suddenly the mood changes, and the attention is switched from sky to earth:

> *No wonder of it: shéer plód makes plough down sillion*
> *Shine, and blue-bleak embers, ah my dear,*
> *Fall, gall themselves, and gash gold-vermilion.*

The poet is saying that it is no wonder that fire breaks from the wonderful bird as it turns and dives, since there are so many beauties in nature: ordinary ploughing of a field makes the earth shine in the furrows (sillions), and when logs fall in a grate they split apart (gall themselves) and produce a lovely colour, a cross between gold and vermilion-red. The windhover, therefore, is just a spectacular example of something which is found everywhere in nature, if only it is perceived and noted. And the poem ends with such a perception. It is a reminder, if one were needed, of the sharp sight and tender mind of the poet, he who perceived the shining earth and the colour of falling logs. He is the same poet who thrilled to the windhover with 'I caught' as the opening words of the poem: and it is his heart which 'in hiding/Stirred for a bird'. The poem is about the heart, its instinctive greeting of the bird in an intuitive understanding, a moment of thrilling excitement at the wonder and power of the natural world. The heart to Hopkins was extremely important: 'What we call heart,' he wrote in one of his sermons, 'is not the piece of flesh so called, not the great bloodvessel only but the thoughts of the mind that vessel seems to harbour and the feelings of the soul to which it beats. For the heart is of all the members of the body the one which most strongly and most of its own accord sympathises with and expresses in itself what goes on within the soul. Tears are sometimes forced, smiles may be put on, but the beating of the heart is the truth of nature.'

If the beating of the heart is the truth of nature, the stirring of the heart for a bird is the leaping of joy of a heart 'in hiding'; that is, a heart which is quickly hidden away within the breast, perhaps because it has not been so stirred for some time. The joy at the sight of the hawk is a joy which is exceptional, and not surprisingly the heart is stirred from its usual slumber. There is no need, in my view, to interpret 'The Windhover' as a poem of tension between Hopkins' natural self and his religious self: the mood of the poem is one of undoubted joy and of unusual excitement, but that need not necessarily mean that Hopkins was habitually depressed, inhibited or frustrated by his life with the Jesuits. Similarly, there is no need to read elaborate symbolism into the last three lines. Hopkins is talking about honest and unremarkable work ('shéer plód') leading to beauty, and unnoticed humble things (embers in a fire) producing lovely colours. It is a mistake, I think, to see this as an emblem of Christ's life, beautiful in destruction. Similarly, there is much pother about the hawk, in its moment of buckling to dive, as a destroyer. Again, this creates an unnecesssary complication; and although literary criticism thrives on complications, it ought not to do so at the expense of the spirit and tone of a poem. If the poem is about Christ's presence in the world, and I think it is, then it is about his presence in beauty and in fear, in flight and ecstasy and destruction, in humility and self-sacrifice as well as in achievement and mastery.

6. Creation, Destruction and Religion: Poems 1877–9

'Pied Beauty' and 'Hurrahing in Harvest'

The naturalness of Hopkins' technique, and the perception of inscape and instress, are seen to great effect in 'Pied Beauty'. It is a poem which is designed to alert the reader to the ordinary beauties of the natural world, and especially the variety of it, the unregarded loveliness of a chestnut ('chestnuts as bright as coals or spots of vermilion' JP 189), or a trout, or freckles. The first line in particular has an undoubted charm, because it links the impressive opening ('Glory be to God') to the simplicity of 'dappled things'. They follow in no particular order: all is 'dappled' or 'pied' within the poem itself as one thing follows another, and everything in the poem is valuable because it contradicts sameness, routine, dullness. The poem is a Curtal Sonnet, or short sonnet: it is on a smaller scale than the usual sonnet of 8 + 6 lines (octave and sestet) and is proportionately smaller at 6 + 4 with a half-line appended. The result is a poem which is short and crisp, filled with images of variety, liveliness and difference. Like its successor, 'Hurrahing in Harvest' (dated 1 September 1877), it is a poem of undisturbed beauty and harmony, because the mind of the writer, praising God for this creation, is in tune with the external world. It is, by its very observation of precise and undervalued features of nature demonstrating its love and praise. The difference between the Curtal Sonnet of 'Pied Beauty' and the full sonnet of 'Hurrahing in Harvest' is not just in size. 'Hurrahing in Harvest' is more complex linguistically and thematically, developing the simple 'Praise him' of 'Pied Beauty' into the idea of the meeting of the human and the divine. The Saviour is in the landscape: his presence is found in the beautiful September skies (where it is 'gleaned' by the poet) and in the 'azurous hung hills' which (shaped like the shoulder of a man)

> *. . . are his world-wielding shoulder*
> *Majestic –*

And when this is recognized, the heart leaps for joy, to such an extent that it

> *réars wings bold and bolder*
> *And hurls for him, O half hurls earth for him off under his feet.*

The great perception strikes him so forcibly that it half throws him off balance; the last line is characteristic of the sonnet's method in its use of repetition:

> *... hurls for him, O half hurls earth for him ...*

The sonnet uses this device in many places. Its characteristic mode is one of a repetition which is also an amplification:

> *Summer ends now: now, barbarous in beauty, the stooks rise ...*
> *I walk, I lift up, I lift up heart, eyes, ...*
> *And, éyes, heárt, what looks, what lips yet gave ...*
> *of realer, of rounder replies ...*

The 'now' of the first line is also important. Hopkins is often the poet of the present tense, using it to give the impression of immediacy (as in the word 'Buckle' in 'The Windhover'). Here the language is pushed to its limits: 'I walk'; 'I lift up'. The verbs sound like a grammar-book for the teaching of English as a foreign language. The lifting *up* of the heart and eyes then contrasts with the *down* of

> *Down all that glory in the heavens to glean our Saviour;*

it is as though the eye travels *down* the sky, suggesting a huge expanse of sky like a field: hence the heart and eyes 'glean' (pick up the remains of) our Saviour. As in 'The Starlight Night', the suggestion is that behind the physical appearance is a much greater reality: what we see of the Saviour in the beauty of the sky are but the gleanings of a much greater harvest.

The images of nature are also very daring in this poem. The stooks are 'barbarous' in their beauty, that is they have a wild, primitive beauty; the clouds are 'silk-sack', as though made of silken sacks, yet also 'Meal-drift', fragments drifting across the sky like meal. They are making waves of cloud in a wilful manner (without set arrangement) and so are 'wilful-wavier' (rhyming, with unusual freedom for Hopkins, with 'be-haviour'). The two compounds seem to go together, multiplying their meanings as they interact 'wilful-wavier/Meal-drift' (wilfully drifting wavy meal; wilfully waving, drifting like meal); and then comes the verb, 'moulded ever'. Hopkins does *not* say 'has it ever moulded' but 'moulded ever'. This not only gives emphasis to 'ever' – has it moulded *ever*? – but it also allows 'ever' to have a double function: it can refer back to 'moulded' and forward to 'melted'. The words are similar, 'mould' giving rise to the echo of 'melt'; but the idea is quite different, an opposition between the clouds forming and then melting away. The clouds mould, and then melt: the Creation is wonderfully changeable and ever-changing.

These and other images demonstrate Hopkins' sense of the external world and its beauty at harvest-time. But the sonnet has another very important structural principle: it is the principle of interaction between two forces, described here as 'behaviour' and likened to manners. The silk-sack clouds in the first quatrain demonstrate a 'lovely behaviour'. The natural response of good manners to this would be good behaviour back. Similarly, in the second quatrain, the heart and eyes lift up, and are given a greeting in response, a greeting akin to the greetings of love but even finer:

> *And, éyes, heárt, what looks, what lips yet gave you a*
> *Rapturous love's greeting of realer, of rounder replies?*

The problem, as the sestet of the sonnet makes clear, is that there is not usually anyone to see these things and relate to them: the good manners, the 'real' and 'round' (rounded, or complete) reply may be seen and felt by the poet, but most of the time the beholder is wanting. When the beholder *is* present to engage in that marvellous intercourse with nature, then the effect is like being thrown off one's feet.

Both 'Pied Beauty' and 'Hurrahing in Harvest' are concerned with beauty. It is seen by Hopkins as related to two parts of the Holy Trinity: God the Father, as Creator ('Pied Beauty') and God the Son, the Incarnate Word who became flesh. In so doing he became a part of creation, and is found *in* creation ('Hurrahing in Harvest'). It is easy to see that for Hopkins the beauty of the world was associated with God and Christ; un-beauty, whether through neglect, or indifference, or destruction, was the work of the devil. Ugliness, dreariness, baseness, were all elements in the world which were against God in Hopkins' religion of beauty: this idea sorted well with his fastidious temperament. In answer to the question which he posed as a title, 'To what serves Mortal Beauty?', he replied emphatically, like a preacher determined to make his point:

> *'See: it does this: keeps warm*
> *Men's wits to the things that are; '* what good means –

The answer is so straightforward that it is in danger of being overlooked. Beauty, quite simply, tells us 'what good means', and indicates what reality is ('the things that are'). It is not surprising, therefore, that throughout the poems of this period, Hopkins was preoccupied with the relationship between human beings and nature. Nature he saw as beautiful and well-mannered, and human beings were often coarse, unfeeling or indifferent. Either they did not notice the beauty around them, or they actually destroyed it (as described in 'Binsey Poplars').

This is because they are too often preoccupied with their own restless and relentless activity, as in 'The Caged Skylark':

> . . . *in drudgery, day-labouring-out life's age.*

'The Caged Skylark'

This poem, 'The Caged Skylark', begins with a suggestion (from Platonic or Neo-Platonic philosophy) that the spirit of man is imprisoned in the body, as a skylark is 'scanted' (given scanty room to live) even though it may have turf and a perch in its cage. The free skylark ('sweet-fowl, song-fowl'), on the other hand, sings easily as it drops down to its wild nest. Hopkins goes on to draw a conclusion, not an easy one:

> *Man's spirit will be flesh-bound when found at best,*
> *But uncumberèd: meadow-down is not distressed*
> *For a rainbow footing it nor he for his bónes rísen.*

In other words, man is necessarily flesh-bound, chained to his body; but at his best he will be spiritual man, unburdened by flesh. He will have conquered the flesh, and undergone a kind of death and resurrection, the death of the old self and the resurrection of the new ('his bónes rísen'). When he is in this state, man is as little distressed by his body as a meadow is by the touch of a rainbow's end. He has escaped from the cage of the body into the freedom of the spirit, and when he does so his songs are no longer 'bursts of fear and rage' but his natural sweet and wild song.

'In the Valley of the Elwy'

This may be the case in theory and religious practice. But Hopkins knew that in the world of ordinary human affairs, beauty was habitually neglected and undervalued. In what looks like a peculiarly 'split' sonnet, 'In the Valley of the Elwy' (in which the octave seems to deal with one subject and the sestet with another), Hopkins describes a kind and good household, where the sweet smell of burning wood corresponds to the sweet nature of the people. In the sestet he continues:

> *Lovely the woods, waters, meadows, combes, vales,*
> *All the air things wear that build this world of Wales;*
> *Only the inmate does not correspond:*

By this he means that the beauty of Wales is not in tune with the Welsh people, so that the beauty is unregarded. As he told Bridges:

As the sweet smell to those kind people so the Welsh landscape is NOT to the Welsh; and the author and principle of all four terms is asked to bring the sum right. (LB 76–7)

The 'four terms' which make up 'the sum' are therefore: the sweet smell, the kind people, the Welsh landscape and the Welsh people. The final prayer to 'bring the sum right' is:

> *God, lover of souls, swaying considerate scales,*
> *Complete thy creature dear O where it fails,*
> *Being mighty a master, being a father and fond.*

Hopkins' feeling about the Welsh is unhappily expressed in this sonnet: to say that the landscape is beautiful but the people do not correspond implies that the people are not mindful of beauty, which is a monstrous generalization. It may have been due, however, to Hopkins' regret that Wales was not Roman Catholic. He longed to do something for the conversion of Wales (JP 258), and his sycophantic poem on the silver jubilee of the first Roman Catholic Bishop of Shrewsbury ends with a reference to

> *her whose velvet vales*
> *Should have pealed with welcome, Wales,*

which is an obtrusive grumble. This unfortunate reminder of heresy (from a Roman Catholic point of view) in Britain occurs again in 'The Loss of the Eurydice'.

'The Loss of the Eurydice'

This is another shipwreck poem, about a vessel which went down off the Isle of Wight in March 1878; but it has little resemblance to 'The Wreck of the Deutschland'. It is written in simple four-line stanzas, rhyming A A B B, in sprung rhythm, with four stresses in lines 1, 2 and 4 and three stresses in line 3 (as usual, the indentation makes this clear); and, as in other places, the stanzas (according to Hopkins' instructions) were to be read as a continuous line: 'The scanning runs on without break to the end of the stanza, so that each stanza is rather one long line rhymed in passage than four lines with rhymes at the ends.' (Poems, p. 223) The emphasis, too, is on the poem's sound: 'you must not slovenly read it with the eyes,' he told Bridges, 'but with your ears, as if the paper were declaiming it at you. For instance the line "She had come from a cruise, training seamen" read without stress and declaim is mere Lloyd's Shipping Intelligence; properly read it is quite a different thing. Stress is the life of it.' (L B 51–2)

The line which Hopkins quoted is an example of the surprising simplicity and directness which he is capable of achieving. In this poem it sits uneasily beside such things as the complicated description of the storm, so that it seems as though the poem has no settled decorum or appropriate style:

> he
> *Came equipped, deadly-electric,*
>
> *A beetling baldbright cloud thorough England*
> *Riding: there did storms not mingle? and*
> *Hailropes hustle and grind their*
> *Heavengravel? wolfsnow, worlds of it, wind there?*

It is possible, of course, to see the two languages as deliberately contrasted. The simplicity of 'She had come from a cruise' may represent a straightforward return voyage that is threatened and finally shipwrecked by the storm; while the complexity of the storm description may mark the way in which the storm gathers destructive powers to itself, just as the language gathers its compounds ('baldbright', 'hailropes', 'heavengravel', 'wolfsnow') and mixes them together with the physical verbs ('hustle', 'grind'). The poem reconstructs the movement of the storm across the Isle of Wight, until the moment of its striking the ship. Then the response is dramatic, with a contrast between two voices, that of the commentator and that of a sailor:

> *Too proud, too proud, what a press she bore!*
> *Royal, and all her royals wore.*
> *Sharp with her, shorten sail!*
> *Too late; lost; gone with the gale.*

Blown over by the wind, the ship turned on its side, so that water rushed in through the open portholes and the ship herself became a death-trap, and

> *. . . she who had housed them thither*
> *Was around them, bound them or wound them with her.*

Hopkins describes one of them, a dead seaman 'of lovely manly mould', and it is at this point that he is led into a distracting passage about those who die outside the Roman Catholic church (lines 85–104). The reader's sympathies up to this point have been engaged with the human tragedy; now Hopkins turns the poem into a discourse about heretics and what happens to them. Not only that; the thought of the sailors 'in / Unchrist, all rolled in ruin' sends him back to deplore the Reformation, with the monasteries destroyed and the shrines unvisited (89–92). He suggests that he might have been able to forgive this ('I might let bygones be') but for the fact that the seamen are now automatically damned; and he wonders how God allowed it to happen –

> *The riving off that race*
> *So at home, time was, to his truth and grace*
>
> *That a starlight-wender of ours would say*
> *The marvellous Milk was Walsingham Way*
> *And one – but let be, let be:*

The 'riving off' is the tearing or rending of the English nation from the Roman church; it was a nation that had at one time been so 'at home' with it that a man walking at night ('a starlight-wender') would have called the Milky Way by a religious name. 'In Catholic times,' Hopkins told Bridges, 'Walsingham Way was a name for the Milky Way, as being supposed a fingerpost to our Lady's shrine at Walsingham.' (LB 53) Such a nostalgia for pre-Reformation times is out of keeping with the wider human sympathies of the poem, and it introduces a note of obsessive concern with the supposed evils of the Protestant religion.

The language of the whole poem is severely compressed, and in the final stanzas this compression becomes something of a liability, for it prevents the meaning from emerging clearly:

> *O well wept, mother have lost son;*
> *Wept, wife; wept, sweetheart would be one: . . .*
>
> *But to Christ lord of thunder*
> *Crouch; lay knee by earth low under:*
> * 'Holiest, loveliest, bravest,*
> *Save my hero, O Hero savest . . .*

There are a number of omissions of relative pronouns and articles here, and these need to be supplied for the lines to make sense. The first line's 'well wept', too, is abrupt. It means, said Hopkins, 'you do well to weep', as in 'well caught' or 'well run' at cricket (LB 53). So these verses mean: 'You do well to weep, O mother who may have lost a son; you do well to weep, O wife; you do well to weep, sweetheart who wished to be one (i.e.

a wife, or perhaps wished to be 'made one' with your sweetheart in marriage); you are to bow down to Christ, the lord of thunder, and kneel; then pray to Him who is holiest, loveliest and bravest, saying "O Christ, Hero who savest, save my own hero."' The abbreviation is awkward here, although Hopkins defended it vigorously against Bridges' criticism, which he described as 'water of the lower Isis' (lower Thames water, or bilge) (LB 54). However, it is difficult to feel that Hopkins was right.

'The May Magnificat'

Another poem of this period which Bridges disliked, principally because he was unsympathetic to Hopkins' religion, was 'The May Magnificat'. Here the association between beauty and Roman Catholicism is made explicit, for the description of May as a beautiful spring month is subordinated to the idea that it is 'Mary's month'. There are some lovely verses, in Hopkins' best combination of acute observation and appropriate diction:

> *When drop-of-blood-and-foam-dapple*
> *Bloom lights the orchard-apple*
> *And thicket and thorp are merry*
> *With silver-surfèd cherry.*
>
> *And azuring-over greyball makes*
> *Wood banks and brakes wash wet like lakes*
> *And magic cuckoocall*
> *Caps, clears, and clinches all —*

But at other points of the poem the relationship between Hopkins the poet and Hopkins the priest seems out of balance: there is no reason why the beauty of May should be seen through the filter of Mariolatry.

'Duns Scotus's Oxford'

The balance between religion and nature is better preserved in 'Duns Scotus's Oxford', a poem of March 1879, although even here the poem moves from the beauty of the scene to the life and work of the theologian. But the octave of the sonnet is less concerned with religion and more expressive of a concern that beauty is disappearing. Oxford, says Hopkins, is lovely, but once it was even lovelier, a place where town and country used to meet. Now —

Thou hast a base and brickish skirt there, sours
That neighbour-nature thy grey beauty is grounded
Best in; graceless growth, thou hast confounded
Rural rural keeping – folk, flocks, and flowers.

The complaint is a typical Victorian one: the idea that the Middle Ages, with their colleges and cathedrals, were somehow more beautiful and spiritual than the nineteenth century was common. Hopkins' description of this is fresh and unusual, but as an insight it is commonplace: to criticize the building of suburbs is to ignore many of the necessary conditions of life. But Hopkins prefers to shut his eyes to this problem, and reflect that

> *. . . this air I gather and I release*
> *He lived on;*

'He' is Duns Scotus, who is thought to have worked in Oxford around 1300; and in reflecting that now he is breathing the same Oxford air, Hopkins is detaching himself from the present and trying to put himself in contact with the spirit of Scotus. Scotus was a brilliant philosopher and theologian,

> *Of realty the rarest-veinèd unraveller; a not*
> *Rivalled insight, be rival Italy or Greece;*
> *Who fired France for Mary without spot.*

As a philosopher, Scotus unravels the nature of things ('realty' or reality) and as a theologian he inspired Roman Catholic France, 'fired' it for Mary 'without spot' (for Mary the *Virgin*, and hence for the Roman church). Hopkins is instinctively remembering the Middle Ages, not just as a time when Oxford was beautiful, but as a time when Europe was Roman Catholic: and this desire to preserve Oxford as some kind of medieval fossil, without suburbs, is connected with his desire to go back to a time before the Reformation. The beauty of Oxford is still there, but faded: it is a symbol of the decline of religion (as Hopkins saw it) in England.

'Binsey Poplars'

His prejudices and assumptions are difficult to take seriously, and Hopkins is on much surer ground in 'Binsey Poplars', where the focusing intelligence is human and not parsonical. It is about the destruction of a row of poplar trees on the river bank near Oxford in 1879, and the act speaks for itself: Hopkins does not need to labour the point. But the particular insight of 'Binsey Poplars' is Hopkins' own development of this: when the poplars were there, it was a 'Sweet especial rural scene'. The crucial word is 'especial', which indicates that it was somewhere unique, a place with its own beautiful character, an individual place; now it has been destroyed. The 'haecceitas' or 'thisness' of the place has gone, and no one will ever see it again. It is a complete loss of something which was part of the beauty of the world, and which has now disappeared for ever. Hopkins emphasizes the finality and brutality of it all by the repetitions in the third line:

> *My aspens dear, whose airy cages quelled*
> *Quelled or quenched in leaves the leaping sun,*
> *All felled, felled, are all felled;*

They are '*my* aspens dear', which immediately gives the poem an impact through its sense of personal loss; and the light movement which follows through the syllables of the first two lines suggests animation and delight. It is into this that the strokes of 'felled, felled, . . . felled' come: they enact the destruction through the rhythm and feel of the verse. They contrast brilliantly not only with the sound of the earlier lines, but with the sense: the image of the 'airy cages' (the branches as bars) catching or quenching the leaping sun is only one of the active, purposeful moments: the trees were 'a fresh and following folded rank', and they seemed to be full of gentle movement:

> *Not spared, not one*
> *That dandled a sandalled*
> *Shadow that swam or sank*
> *On meadow and river . . .*

The image of the tree 'dandling' a shadow, as a mother dandles a baby, suggests life, health, gentleness, rocking, movement. The shadows themselves swim or sink (remain on the surface or dive underneath, like swimmers); the shadows themselves seem active, light-footed ('sandalled'). Hopkins is here attempting, very successfully, to translate the visual patterns of light and movement into words. The whole of the first verse is given up to this free and fresh movement, except for the terrible third line, and the reminder in the fifth ('Not spared, not one').

The second verse turns from this initial contrast to become reflective, but again the aggressive sounds are used to contrast with the living natural world:

> *O if we but knew what we do*
> *When we delve or hew –*
> *Hack and rack the growing green!*

'Delve' (dig) and 'hew' (cut with an axe) are words for necessary country practices, but they give rise in Hopkins' mind to another pair 'Hack and rack'. This pair suggests torture, and the contrast between 'rack' and 'growing green' (suggesting youth and tenderness) is extreme. The idea of tenderness is important in this verse. 'Country' (Hopkins' word for nature, or for the countryside, characteristically unexpected) 'is so tender' and is also 'slender' (another unexpected word, suggesting something very vulnerable, and connected with 'growing': the image is of a slender, growing child being attacked by someone much stronger). These images of torture and brutality reach a climax with the comparison:

> *That, like this sleek and seeing ball*
> *But a prick will make no eye at all,*

The ball is the eyeball, and the frightful image is of a needle or dart going into the eye and blinding someone. Putting out someone's eyes has always seemed a most terrible cruelty (as it is, for instance, in Shakespeare's *King Lear*), and here the parallel is clear and frightening: cutting down the trees is as violent an act towards nature, as cruel and final, as putting a needle into someone's eye would be to a human being. Hopkins' imagination here is tumbling out an image of such ferocious painfulness that it almost seems excessive: yet it serves to prevent the poem from being just a reflection on the preservation of rural England. Hopkins really does see the process as destruction, pain and torture: the blows of the axe, the sharp edge of the blade, are cutting in to something living, tender, harmless, good, gentle.

Sometimes these tree-fellings, or other alterations, are done with the best of intentions. So 'even when we mean/To mend her we end her' and the result is that no one will ever see that beauty again. At times the destruction seems casual as well as quick:

> *Ten or twelve, only ten or twelve*
> *Strokes of havoc únselve*
> *The sweet especial scene,*

The 'ten or twelve' are, of course, the strokes of the axe: the indeterminate number suggests that sometimes the tree falls after a few strokes, and sometimes it needs a few more; while the repetition enacts the way the strokes seem to go on and on, either at one tree or on to the next one. At the same time the arithmetic sounds casual, careless, as though the axe-wielder did not care how many strokes it took. What the strokes do is a kind of murder: they 'unselve' the scene. They destroy its *self*, its essence, its particular individuality. As in 'As kingfishers catch fire . . .' each thing 'Selves – goes itself', so here the woodman 'únselves' the scene. To 'self' is the most valuable thing that a creature can do: it is to 'be', to be itself; and here the felling of the trees leaves no self. Nothing is left of the scene which was both 'special' and 'rural', and the past is evoked sadly in the lovely counterpoint at the end of the poem:

> *The sweet especial scene,*
> *Rural scene, a rural scene,*
> *Sweet especial rural scene.*

Under the heading of 'people and places' I have grouped together five poems which demonstrate Hopkins' art in a particularly pure form. They are 'The Bugler's First Communion', 'Henry Purcell', 'Felix Randal', 'Inversnaid' and 'Ribblesdale'. The first two were written during Hopkins' not very happy time as a priest in Oxford during 1879; 'Felix Randal' was written in Liverpool in April 1880; 'Inversnaid' (a place on the east side of Loch Lomond) dates from a visit to Scotland in 1881, and 'Ribblesdale' from the return to Stonyhurst (which is in the Ribble valley, in Lancashire) in 1882.

Each poem is different from the others, but they have this in common: by describing a particular person or place as accurately as possible, they demonstrate Hopkins' search for the essential individuality of each one. In form, diction, metre and tone, each has its own inscape, its own particular way of selving, of speaking itself; and this reflects Hopkins' awareness of the individuality of the subject-matter, the separateness of each person, or place, or moment.

'The Bugler's First Communion'

'The Bugler's First Communion' is one of Hopkins' rare poems about his priestly office ('Felix Randal' is another). It describes the boy bugler coming to Father Hopkins for Holy Communion, which he had requested when Hopkins was visiting Cowley Barracks. Hopkins feels all the delight of the priest who is being given the opportunity to fulfil his proper function (stanza 3), and he idealizes the young soldier as 'Breathing bloom of a chastity in mansex fine'. At the moment when he kneels, the boy seems touchingly noble, and touchingly vulnerable: Hopkins prays that other soldiers, angels, will march beside him to destroy the forces ('the hell-rook ranks') which sally forth to molest him. Whimsically, yet pleasingly, Hopkins sees himself as, in his way, giving out the rations (only this sacrament is 'Christ's royal ration'); and for a moment he enjoys a perfect relationship with the boy, as giver to receiver, priest to bugler. His prayers are for such good to continue, but he knows that there are many pitfalls for the young man: indeed, he wishes to see him no more, in case disappointment would

Those sweet hopes quell whose least me quickenings lift,

that is, end those hopes, the least quickenings of which lift me – of seeing one day a modern Sir Galahad (Galahad was the purest of Arthur's knights of the Round Table, the one who was allowed to see the Holy Grail). All he, as the boy's priest, can do, is to pray, and his prayers are uttered with all his power. He can only trust in God, and record that he has spoken pleas (which)

> *Would brandle adamantine heaven with ride and jar, did*
> > *Prayer go disregarded:*
> *Forward-like, but however, and like favourable heaven heard these.*

'Brandle' means 'shake'; and Hopkins is suggesting that his prayer is of such force that it would shake heaven if it were ignored. His prayer is 'forward', that is 'pressing forward, or urgent', and the first half of the final line needs to be reversed to be understood: 'But it is urgent, however, and it is likely ('like' = 'belike') that favourable heaven *did* hear these pleas.'

The poem is strangely effective in its tangled way. Its difficulty arises from the fact that Hopkins is handling material of great delicacy and sanctity: in particular the feelings of a priest on giving communion to a young soldier. The poem is also a description of prayer, which is itself a devotional practice of some intensity. Yet what the complicated language and syntax does is to unite the circumstance – the soldier, the priest, the wafer ('leaf light housel') – with the aspiration – the hope for the future, the misgivings, the prayer – into a dense and complex poem about life and religion.

'Henry Purcell'

'Henry Purcell' is also a difficult poem, and for a similar reason: Hopkins is attempting to describe something very individual and complex. In this case there is a prefatory note, which is presumably supposed to explain the poem but which is not at all easy:

The poet wishes well to the divine genius of Purcell and praises him that, whereas other musicians have given utterance to the moods of man's mind, he has, beyond that, uttered in notes the very make and species of man as created both in him and in all men generally.

This statement refers, I think, to Hopkins' ideas of inscape and instress. Purcell's music does not merely reflect moods (of himself and others): it gives expression to the very 'man-ness' of man, the 'haecceitas' or special thisness of what is meant by man. So Purcell's music, which is the 'forgèd feature' (line 7) 'finds' the poet, discovers him for what he is:

> *it is the rehearsal*
> *Of own, of abrúpt sélf there so thrusts on, so throngs the ear.*

The ear is surprised by the 'rehearsal' (the repetition or 'going through') of the 'own self', the sudden, immediate self ('abrúpt sélf') which thrusts itself upon the ear and fills it.

In a letter to Bridges, Hopkins thought it necessary to summarize the meaning of the sonnet. Bridges had clearly had some difficulty with it, because Hopkins added 'it is somewhat dismaying to find I am so unintelligible though, especially in one of my very best pieces' (LB 171). His summary was brief:

1–4. I hope Purcell is not damned for being a Protestant, because I love his genius. 5–8. And that not so much for gifts he shares, even though it shd. be in higher measure, with other musicians as for his own individuality. 9–14. So that while he is aiming only at impressing me his hearer with the meaning in hand I am looking out meanwhile for his specific, his individual markings and mottlings, 'the sakes of him'.

Conscious that the first lines caused particular difficulty, Hopkins then went on to unravel them in more detail:

In particular, the first lines mean: May Purcell, O may he have died a good death and that soul which I love so much and which breathes or stirs so unmistakeably in his works have parted from the body and passed away, centuries since though I frame the wish, in peace with God! (LB 170–71)

The first line continued to cause problems, and Hopkins refers to it in two further letters (28 January and 3 February 1883). The key to it is the knowledge that 'Have fair fallen' means may good have befallen such a special ('especial', as we have seen in 'Binsey Poplars' was an important word for Hopkins, and Purcell is '*arch*-especial', like 'archbishop') spirit as is found in Henry Purcell. He is such a dear spirit to me, even though an age has passed since he parted (de-parted = died); may this be accompanied by a reversal of the sentence (of damnation) that lays him low ('low lays him') because he was on earth ('here') enlisted ('listed') to a heresy (that is, he lived and died a Protestant).

As a summary, this sounds unnecessarily, even disagreeably, preoccupied with Purcell and Protestantism: read as Hopkins wrote it, the first quatrain has its own remarkable and expressive quality, with the rhythm and alliteration producing a sense of deep feeling and apprecia-

103

tion. It is a good example of the way in which Hopkins' poetry does not gain from paraphrase. Similarly, the second quatrain is its own individual rendering of the idea which is stated in the prefatory note: it is not the *mood* of Purcell's music, or his *meaning* that matters, or his love or pity, or anything that other musicians might be able to write ('all that sweet notes not his might nursle' = foster). It is, as we have seen, the essential self, the 'very make and species' of man, which 'finds' the poet, seeks out his inner selfhood.

The poet attempts to develop this, but in a letter shortly after the poem's composition he admits that 'the sestet of the Purcell sonnet is not so clearly worked out as I could wish' (LB 83). It begins with the hope that the spirit of Purcell 'with his air of angels' (his 'air' in the sense of music, perhaps, but also in the sense of manner – 'his angelic manner') would 'lift me' (inspire) and 'lay me' (be my rest, lay me down to rest); whatever happens the poet will 'Have an eye to the sakes of him' (that is, he will have an eye for his distinctive quality of genius: see the discussion of 'sake' above, pp. 44–5). At this point the sonnet switches abruptly to the image of the stormfowl, even before the act of comparison is signalled (after the semi-colon, by 'so'). The 'moonmarks' are 'crescent-shaped markings on the quill-feathers' (LB 83), which are seen beneath the wings when the bird flies. The comparison is explained *after* the image of moonmarks, plumage and wings: the poet, we discover, is thinking of 'some great stormfowl', which has been walking on a sea-beach, on a day of purple thunderclouds. When it flies it makes a rushing of wind ('wuthering') and the movement of the wings seems curved like a giant smile; but the beholders wonder afresh at it each time. Hopkins summarized it thus:

The thought is that as the seabird opening his wings with a whiff of wind in your face means the whirr of the motion, but also unaware gives you a whiff of knowledge about his plumage, the marking of which stamps his species, that he does not mean, so Purcell, seemingly intent only on the thought or feeling he is to express or call out, incidentally lets you remark the individualising marks of his own genius. (LB 83)

The sophistication of all this is difficult enough in prose: Hopkins' idea that the conscious purpose is less important than the incidental revelation is difficult to express and not easy for the reader to tease out. It is worth trying to understand it, however: Hopkins is describing that inner 'core' of a person's art, the essence which gives it its own stamp and individuality. It is this which seems more central, more touching, more 'finding', that which speaks from the centre.

Perhaps because it is so concerned with an intimate and inner feeling, that essence of a musician's art which 'finds' the listener, 'Henry Purcell' has its own intimate language to match, full of quaint and individual constructions, with unusual words and idiosyncratic meanings.

'Felix Randal'

'Felix Randal' is very different. Its ideas are much more accessible and traditional, and its language is more straightforward, though wonderfully vigorous and energetic. It is a poem about a farrier, or blacksmith; it reflects on his dying, his last illness, the priest's compassion for him and on his former strength; it is a poem which stirs echoes of the Psalms, with their moving recognition of man's mortality:

As for man, his days are as grass: as a flower of the field, so he flourisheth.
For the wind passeth over it, and it is gone; and the place thereof shall know it no more. (Psalm 103:15–16)

In the same way, the poet contrasts the last feeble days of the farrier with his earlier years, before death or sickness were ever 'forethought of':

How far from then forethought of, all thy more boisterous years,
When thou at the random grim forge, powerful amidst peers,
Didst fettle for the great grey drayhorse his bright and battering sandal!

These lines emphasize Felix's strength in a number of different ways. A word such as 'boisterous' suggests an abundance of energy, a noisy and almost wild enjoyment of life; at the forge, too, Felix was powerful among other powerful men, part of the whole scene – the forge, built of random or rough stone, the powerful men, the big horses. The fact that Felix was able to 'fettle' (make ready) the horseshoe for the 'great grey drayhorse' suggests his competence and strength. The whole vocabulary lends itself to this: the force of words such as 'farrier', 'forge' and 'fettle', and the technical words such as 'random' and 'drayhorse' suggest a world apart, a world of craftsmanship and strength. Indeed, the poem's main structural principle is the contrast between the strength of Felix, 'big-boned and hardy-handsome' and his weakness, in which he first of all cursed and then turned to religion and was comforted by the priest.

Hopkins as priest is important in this poem, as he was in 'The Bugler's First Communion'. The two poems are, in part, about his work, his life, and his duty. The word 'duty' comes in the first line:

Felix Randal the farrier, O is he dead then? my duty all ended,

This is the priest at his work, in conversation with someone who has just brought him the news: 'Felix Randal is dead.' 'Felix Randal, the farrier, O is he dead then?' By putting the first line in its conversational context it can be seen how natural it is in expression and idea. It can be seen, too, how quickly the necessary information is packed in to that first line; ending with 'my duty all ended', which indicates that the speaker is a priest, Father Hopkins. And the sonnet could be said to be about two kinds of work: the blacksmith, using his strength at the forge, and the priest, doing his work among the sick and dying with another kind of strength. For, as the Psalmist knew, physical strength cannot last:

> *Sickness broke him. Impatient, he cursed at first, but mended*
> *Being anointed and all; though a heavenlier heart began some*
> *Months earlier, since I had our sweet reprieve and ransom*
> *Tendered to him. Ah well, God rest him all road ever he offended!*

The 'sweet reprieve and ransom' is the sacrament of Holy Communion, which carries with it the promise of forgiveness and new life. The phrase 'Being anointed and all' is touchingly colloquial, as 'all road' is subsequently; both are part of a pattern in this verse, in which the speaking voice almost overrides the rhythm and turns the lines into prose. Hopkins' belief that his art was natural is carried into practice here, in the enjambement of 'a heavenlier heart began some / Months earlier . . .' and in the following phrase 'since I had our sweet reprieve and ransom / Tendered to him'. The unpretentious naturalness of these lines is effective in its simplicity, and very human in its colloquial note; and it is not until the opening of the sestet that the linguistic devices of the craftsman begin to appear again:

> *This seeing the sick endears them to us, us too it endears.*

Here the chiasmus 'endears . . . to . . . us . . . us . . . too . . . endears' gives the impression of having been thought out, reflected upon: the 'to . . . too' is a kind of verbal joke, in which Hopkins finds an unexpected resemblance in sound to correspond with the unexpected human consequence of visiting the sick and dying. It endears the people to the priests, but in the process it brings the priests closer to the people. The two lines which follow are beautifully tender, with their remembrance of speaking ('tongue'), touching with the hand and of Felix's tears touching back in the 'touching' of the priest's heart, followed by the pauses and repetition 'child, Felix, poor Felix Randal'. The counterpoint between 'child' and 'poor' on the one hand and 'Felix . . . Felix Randal' on the other is very delicate and feeling: 'Felix' is 'poor Felix', yet also a child: childlike in his helplessness, and also a child of God in the eyes of the priest. The pauses, the naming and re-naming, and the fall at the end of the line, all register emotion with a most expressive use of language and rhythm.

From this beautiful diminuendo the poem returns at the end to portray Felix in his prime, at work in his forge. From the tender 'poor child' on his deathbed, we return to the farrier fettling the bright and battering sandal. The poem is remarkable, even by Hopkins' standards, in its ability to encompass both portrayals in its language: the sound of the farrier at work in the 't's of the last line and the 'p's of the line before, and the sound of the priest's inner voice – 'child, Felix, poor Felix Randal'.

If 'Henry Purcell' and 'Felix Randal' are two very different poems in subject, tone and treatment, the same can be said of the two place poems, 'Inversnaid' and 'Ribblesdale'. Each has its own technique, which is used for its own proper purpose: and the whole bent and purpose of each poem is unique to that poem. Just as the place itself *is* itself and nowhere else, so the language and inscape of the poem is untransferable: they are not, in other words, a pair of poems about two different landscapes.

'Inversnaid'

'Inversnaid' is an unusual poem for Hopkins, because it is entirely concerned with nature and the landscape and there is no reference to God. Instead, its last verse is a straight plea for the preservation of wildness; and although we can probably deduce that behind this plea there is the idea that untouched nature is of God and spoiled nature is the work of man, it is never given expression in the poem. The poem's interest lies in Hopkins' attempt to describe a Highland stream as exactly as possible, as though that description would be enough: the more the water is described, the more it seems necessary to make sure that it remains as it is. The stream, and the landscape around it, are themselves, and good in themselves:

> *This darksome burn, horseback brown,*
> *His rollrock highroad roaring down,*
> *In coop and in comb the fleece of his foam*
> *Flutes and low to the lake falls home.*

What is noticeable here is the extraordinary care (found also in the notebooks and journals) to get the appearances exactly right. How is the colour of the water to be described? It is the colour of a horse's back. How is its movement to be captured? It is roaring down a highway, but a highroad that is made up of rocks, over which it tumbles and rolls. Looking more closely, it can be seen that the water falls into little enclosed pools so it is 'In coop' or cooped in; and it comes over the rocks in vertical lines, like a comb. Its foam is like the back of a sheep, and then it runs down between the rocks in flutes (like fluting on a pillar: Hopkins compresses it all by saying that the burn 'flutes', turns itself into vertical, rounded shapes) before falling to the lake at the bottom of the slope.

Sometimes the froth is blown up by the wind; it is usually fawn-coloured, and it turns and 'twindles' (twists and dwindles) over the dark pool. The pool stirs round like broth: it is so dark, its blackness is so profound, that as it goes round you could imagine despair itself, black despair, drowning in such blackness.

In the third verse, the dew is found upon the fold ('groins') of the braes: they are 'Degged' (sprinkled) and dappled with it, and so are the 'packs' or clusters of heather, and the 'flitches' (tufts) of fern, together with the mountain ash or rowan tree, the 'beadbonny ash' known for its red berries.

Throughout the poem the alliteration is pronounced and the rhyme scheme assertive: they encourage a vigorous recital, a rapid delivery which reaches a climax in the 'l's and 'w's of the final verse.

'Ribblesdale'

An entirely different language is used in 'Ribblesdale'. No longer is it compressed, exact in reference, alliterative; it is now more relaxed, gentler, more reflective, sweeter:

> Earth, sweet Earth, sweet landscape, with leavès throng
> And louchèd low grass, heaven that dost appeal
> To, with no tongue to plead, no heart to feel;
> That canst but only be, but dost that long –
> Thou cànst but be, but that thou well dost; strong
> Thy plea with him who dealt, nay does now deal,
> Thy lovely dale down thus and thus bids reel
> Thy river, and o'er gives all to rack or wrong.

The meaning of this octave, which is difficult, is clarified by a quotation in the manuscript, from the Epistle to the Romans (8:19–20):

For the earnest expectation of the creature waiteth for the manifestation of the sons of God.
For the creature was made subject to vanity, not willingly, but by reason of him who subjected the same in hope.

The quotation is about a fallen world, subjected to vanity by the power of Satan, and waiting for the revealing of the sons of God, in other words for the second coming, the Day of Judgment, and the triumph of God. So Hopkins portrays Ribblesdale as a landscape appealing mutely to the heavens: it has no tongue and no feeling heart, but nevertheless it does not merely exist, it longs for paradise, for the coming of God. That would indeed make for the perfection which is missing, although the landscape performs its function well as it is: its beauty, although it is the beauty of a fallen world, must give it a strong claim with God, who created it in such loveliness and who watches over the whole world.

The descriptive language of this octave is much less precise than it is in 'Inversnaid'. Here Hopkins uses phrases such as 'sweet landscape' and 'lovely dale'. They are, of course, mixed with other words – 'throng', for example, which Hopkins (identifying with the locality) said was '"throng" for an adjective as we use it here in Lancashire'. Similarly, 'louchèd' for the low grass, meaning slouched or slouching, is probably intended to give life and feeling to the 'sweet earth, sweet landscape' by endowing the grass with life and movement. Yet the dale and the river are not described with any particularity: God the creator is the one

> who dealt, nay does now deal,
> *Thy lovely dale down thus and thus bids reel*
> *Thy river, . . .*

The sestet helps to make things clearer. Since the earth has no tongue to plead, and no heart to feel, it is man who should express its reverence towards God and its longing for Him. But man, 'dear and dogged man', is too busy to bother with such things:

> the heir
> *To his own self bent so bound, so tied to his turn,*
> *To thriftless reave both our rich round world bare*
> *And none reck of world after, . . .*

This is once again the priest's cry for man to turn to God. On this occasion nature is calling out to man to intercede on her behalf with God, but he is preoccupied with what Hopkins sees as (literally) soul-destroying labour. He is so busy with his routine ('tied to his turn') and also committed to 'thriftless reave' (plunder without thought for the future) of the earth that he takes no thought of the next world. Such a state of affairs

> *bids wear*
> *Earth brows of such care, care and dear concern.*

The earth cares for the fate of man, is concerned about him: this is one reason why it looks as it does, and gives the poet the impression that it is somehow longing for the revelation of the sons of God. At the end of the sonnet, therefore, we are returned to the beginning of it.

This return at the end is significant, for it underlines what is so important in this poem. and that is the complex interaction between the perceiving mind and the external world. In 'Ribblesdale'. the interaction is a complicated response; in 'Inversnaid' a fairly simple one. But both demonstrate the way in which Hopkins' poetry is never purely descriptive: it is moral, personal and sometimes religious in its aim and content. The same can be said about the poems concerned with people: 'Henry Purcell' is less about Purcell's music than about its effect upon the poet, and 'Felix Randal', while more concerned to describe the farrier. is also a poem about the office and function of a Roman Catholic priest. All the poems dealt with in this section. therefore, are poems in which there is a central process of relationship, between man and man, or between man and nature.

8. The Terrible Sonnets

'I shall shortly have some sonnets to send you,' Hopkins wrote to Bridges on 1 September 1885, 'five or more':

Four of these came like inspirations unbidden and against my will. And in the life I lead now, which is one of a continually jaded and harassed mind, if in any leisure I try to do anything I make no way   nor with my work, alas! but so it must be. (LB 221)

It is not certain which sonnets were being referred to here, but the usual suggestion is that they are probably:

> 'No worst, there is none . . .'
> 'To seem the stranger . . .'
> 'I wake and feel the fell of dark . . .'
> 'Patience, hard thing! . . .'
> 'My own heart let me more have pity on . . .'

To them should be added 'Carrion Comfort', which may have been the sonnet referred to by Hopkins in a letter to Bridges written earlier in the year: 'I have after long silence written two sonnets . . . if ever anything was written in blood one of these was' (LB 219).

The sonnets are terrible because they are intimate, private and confessional records of the problems attending on a severe religious discipline. As we have seen, Hopkins saw his happiness in self-surrender, and chose the Jesuit Order because the Benedictines would not have suited him. These sonnets are a record of the price that he had to pay. He had hoped to find peace in the total obedience of the Jesuit; but he often found frustration and unhappiness. His preaching was not very successful, and he was not particularly happy in his work as a priest except for a short period at Bedford Leigh in Lancashire; and his appointment as Professor of Classics at University College, Dublin, was not congenial to him. He remembered the promises of Jesus in St John's Gospel (14:16–17): 'And I will pray the Father, and he shall give you another Comforter, that he may abide with you for ever; Even the Spirit of truth.' They did not seem to apply to him:

> *Comforter, where, where is your comforting?*
> 'No worst, there is none . . .'

Both as a professor and a priest he felt himself to be unsuccessful. His classes in Dublin were rude and unresponsive; and as a priest the standards were high and the demands unremitting. 'I have never wavered in my vocation,' he told Dixon, 'but I have not lived up to it.' (LD 88)

The image which recurs in the letters and the poetry of this period is that of the eunuch, as though Hopkins felt that his creativity had been violently cut off: 'it kills me to be time's eunuch and never to beget,' he wrote to Bridges in 1885 (LB 222). 'Nothing comes,' he wrote in 1888: 'I am a eunuch – but it is for the kingdom of heaven's sake.' (LB 270) The image was incorporated into one of the last sonnets, 'Thou art indeed just, Lord . . .':

> . . . *birds build – but not I build; no, but strain,*
> *Time's eunuch, and not breed one work that wakes.*

The association of the failure of creativity with sexual sterility is only one of the many ways in which Hopkins uses physical imagery to describe the horror of his mental condition. He had always used physical images with power ('disappointment and humiliations embitter the heart and make an aching in the very bones' – LD 9), but now the language becomes grotesque and horrifying: when he met the young Irish poet, Katherine Tynan, he told Bridges, 'she took me for 20 and some friend of hers for 15; but it won't do: they should see my heart and vitals, all shaggy with the whitest hair.' (LB 250) Some of this disturbing imagery is responsible for the power and the painful energy of the terrible sonnets, and even of the end of 'Spelt from Sibyl's Leaves' where 'thóughts against thoughts ín groans grínd'. The idea of thoughts grinding against each other, as rough stones might do, is unpleasant to feel and hearing; so too there are images of cries wincing on an anvil ('No worst . . .'), of hearts that 'grate on themselves' ('Patience, hard thing! . . .') and of the self tasting as bitter as heartburn ('I wake and feel . . .').

Hopkins knew the reason for these terrible experiences. They were the price that had to be paid, not only for his self-sacrifice, but also for his sensitive nature. He had written about this in his commentary on the *Spiritual Exercises*:

The keener the consciousness the greater the pain;

The greater the stress of being the greater the pain: both these show that the higher the nature the greater the penalty. (SD 138)

We may see this thought as behind much of the intensity of the terrible sonnets; but what is so remarkable about them is the way in which the poetic language actually seems to recreate the suffering, so that it becomes no longer something in a theory but a bitter experience.

'Carrion Comfort'

In the commentary on the *Spiritual Exercises*, Hopkins speaks at one point of 'the concentration of the mind on the scapes of its own sin' (SD 138). This has a curious double-edged function: 'the instressing of the scope of the sin is a mitigation of pain, and . . . at the same time it is a torment.' (SD 139) It is this kind of subtle contradiction – which is true to experience – that is found in 'Carrion Comfort'. The very title itself faces two ways: Despair is a comfort, yet it is also carrion (a putrefying corpse). The poet is tempted to feast on despair, but instead turns to carry on the wrestling with God. He is at the end of his tether, but refuses to cry *'I can no more'*. He:

> *Can something, hope, wish day come, not choose not to be.*

There are some things which are still possible: the refusal to give up and to commit suicide in despair is one of them. But Hopkins is in no doubt about the effort which is required if he is to carry on. He has to struggle with this terrifying reality, God Himself (as Jacob wrestled with God (Genesis 32:24–30). The imagery of the octave powerfully recreates this physical struggle:

> *. . . O thou terrible, why wouldst thou rude on me*
> *Thy wring-world right foot rock? lay a lionlimb against me? scan*
> *With darksome devouring eyes my bruisèd bones? and fan,*
> *O in turns of tempest, me heaped there; me frantic to avoid thee and flee?*

The reason is stated in the sestet:

> *Why? That my chaff might fly; my grain lie, sheer and clear.*

God is now not just a wrestler, but a thresher: His beating of the poet is like the beating out of corn, and what will be left is only the good and nourishing. And then the poet reflects that it seems to him that '(seems)' since he began the religious life (since he 'kissed the rod', or rather, he says, the *hand* of God, as a courtier kisses hands) during all the toil and fuss ('coil') that followed, his heart has against all the odds 'lapped strength' (as a cat laps milk) and stolen joy, and 'would laugh, chéer'. He is so near the end of his tether now, however, that he ruefully wonders who is cheered: God (the hero, the great wrestler) or himself ('me that fought him'). Was it one, or both? The whole process is a great mystery, and the question is unanswered, for in the last two lines the poet is again overwhelmed with the thought that throughout that whole period of depression he was actually 'wrestling with (my God!) my God'. The insertion of 'my God!' in brackets is extraordinarily daring and colloquial: it is just the sort of exclamation which might have been made by someone confronted with something amazing, and here it retains that meaning; but it also carries with it another meaning, that of recognition. The poet cries 'my God!' as he becomes aware of the extraordinary wonder and mystery of his opponent.

The poem indicates some period of darkness and torment, but it should be remembered that for mystics there is a way to God through desolation and the dark night of the soul, and Hopkins could be said here to be exploring the *via negativa*, the way to God through the 'night, that year/Of now done darkness'. 'Carrion Comfort' is thus strictly not one of the terrible sonnets, in that the poet is aware of the pain as a process of purgation and growth towards God.

'No worst, there is none . . .'

This sonnet is different from 'Carrion Comfort' in tone, rhythm and feeling. It lacks the abundant energy, the forward movement of 'Carrion Comfort', and although some of the images are violent and powerful, it is essentially a poem of a different character. This can be seen immediately in the different grammatical structure of the first lines of each poem: 'Carrion Comfort' begins with a long, twisting sentence which stretches to nearly three lines; 'No worst, there is none . . .' stops dead in the middle of the first line. The pause which results is itself indicative of a certain stillness which is found in this poem, and which suggests exhaustion, or an inability to speak. The only things which have any energy are the pangs: they are 'schooled at forepangs' (taught at the feet of earlier pangs, or perhaps 'instructed at how to give preparatory pangs'). They are 'Pitched past pitch of grief': whatever can be imagined as the 'pitch' or centre of grief, these are beyond it; and they will 'wring' (squeeze out) the poet more wildly than ever. By the use of 'wilder wring' the poet not only provides a physical verb to describe a mental state – here the state of being wrung dry like a wet cloth   but the wringing is done more wildly, as if by someone who has already done the wringing in a frenzy, and is now squeezing and twisting in an even greater fury.

After the two dramatic lines, the cry of the religious, the poem continues with a description of his passionate and desperate cries. We have just had two examples of them, and now 'My cries heave, herds-long':

they go on and on, one after the other, like a herd of cattle; like cattle, too, they 'huddle' or gather together, but when they do so they 'huddle in a main', in a power or strength (from 'might and main'). There they are a 'chief/Woe, wórld-sorrow': they huddle, as it were, into a major sadness, a woe that overspreads the world. As they do so, they 'wince and sing' (associated by sound with the earlier 'wring', and similarly physical verbs), crying out as they are beaten on the anvil of pain. Then, like a storm, the cries 'lull, then leave off'.

This phrase 'Then lull, then leave off' is an exact echo, rhythmically, of the first part of line 1: 'No worst, there is none'. In both cases the line stops short, only to be taken up again, in the first case by the pangs, and now by Fury, who appears like some figure from a Greek myth, a pursuer who shrieks for her victim: 'Let me be fell' (deadly), and 'I must (per-)force be quick about it'.

The Fury appears to be deadly, but in fact the poet survives to meditate upon the landscape of the mind:

> O the mind, mind has mountains; cliffs of fall
> Frightful, sheer, no-man-fathomed.

Hopkins' argument is that to have encountered such cliffs and precipices of the mind is to have acquired a certain authenticity through suffering, an experience from which the poet can draw the conclusion

> Hold them cheap
> May who ne'er hung there.

Such suffering, according to Hopkins (and to some existentialist philosophers) is an indication of true humanity; and the sonnet ends with the very human recognition that no one can stand that kind of misery for very long:

> Nor does long our small
> Durance deal with that steep or deep.

The words 'steep' and 'deep', themselves a powerful reminder of the cliffs and falls of earlier lines, give rise in Hopkins' rhyming mind to the word 'creep'. In turn this suggests creeping under cover, like a hurt animal:

> Here! creep,
> Wretch, under a comfort serves in a whirlwind: all
> Life death does end and each day dies with sleep.

Hopkins may have been thinking of Shakespeare's King Lear, out in the storm, creeping in to whatever shelter he can find with the poor fool and the naked Edgar. In the present case the only comfort is that 'each day dies with sleep': that we lose consciousness at some point, and that, in the end we die and all suffering is over. The inversion 'all/Life death does end' (meaning 'death ends all life', but now emphasizing the 'all') is typical of this sonnet in its twisting and turning of the normal syntax. This gives a sense of strain and tension: it also is part of the poem's astonishing dramatic range, from the spoken cries, 'Comforter...' to the internal musings, and to the final consolation (which is hardly a consolation, more a recognition of the pain and tragedy of the world).

'To seem the stranger...'

'To seem the stranger...' is less obviously dramatic, but it too twists and turns in its exploration of Hopkins' misery and his feeling of exile in Ireland. The phrases are carefully shaped, as in all his poetry, to bring out the full force of the emotion:

> *To seem the stranger lies my lot, my life*
> *Among strangers.*

As in 'Felix Randal' ('This seeing the sick endears them to us, us too it endears') the structure is a chiasmus, a–b–b–a: 'stranger ... lot ... life ... strangers'. In his life, Hopkins says, the lot has fallen to him to seem a stranger to others, and to live among those who are strangers to him (as in 'Felix Randal', the chiasmus brilliantly expresses the movement from the self outwards, and from the external world back to the self). His parents, his brothers and sisters, are not close to him 'in Christ', which means that he feels alone in his Roman Catholicism and his Jesuit calling: this is the first indication that the poem is about something more than just living in Ireland. It is a Jesuit reflecting on his vows of obedience, and what they may have cost him: Christ, who is his peace (according to church teaching, for only in self-surrender can peace come) is also responsible for his parting, for his 'sword and strife' – the wars within him and the trouble that besets him from without. The thought of Ireland and the troubles turns his mind to England:

> *England, whose honour O all my heart woos, wife*
> *To my creating thought, would neither hear*
> *Me, were I pleading, plead nor do I: ...*

Hopkins is remembering the way in which his poetry was written as part of a delighted response to the joy and beauty of nature in England and

Wales (stimulated by the kind of thrilled perception that is found in the notebooks and journals). He knows that England would be indifferent to such pleas, and (being a Jesuit) he must not repine. He merely records his unhappiness:

> ... *I wear-*
> *y of idle a being but by where wars are rife.*

which means 'I am weary of the pointlessness of a life lived only in a place where there is conflict ('wars are rife' refers to the Irish struggle for Home Rule).

The situation becomes clear in the sestet:

> *I am in Ireland now; now I am at a third*
> *Remove.*

The 'third / Remove' is a physical way of describing his feelings of alienation: the first remove was from his family; the second from his peace in Christ; the third from England, where he felt at home. And in spite of the kindness of friends everywhere, his creative impulse has failed: the wisest words which his heart breeds are barred (either by heaven's inscrutable order or by the curse of hell):

> ... *Only what word*
> *Wisest my heart breeds dark heaven's baffling ban*
> *Bars or hell's spell thwarts.*

The poem finishes with two typical Hopkins tricks of rhetoric:

> ... *This to hoard unheard,*
> *Hoard unheeded, leaves me a lonely began.*

The echo and chime of 'hoard-unheard-hoard-unheeded' focuses the mind on the relationship between these words, and on the successive stages of unhappiness: the poet hoards, unheard, and even if he is heard, nobody listens. It is a cry of failure and frustration and it leaves him 'a lonely began' (a beginner). Here the use of the verb's past tense gives a characteristically surprising force to the idea: he feels that he has achieved nothing, and is (in one sense) back where he began.

'I wake and feel ...'

'No worst, there is none ...' had ended by offering the comfort of sleep. 'I wake and feel ...' deals with the worse condition of being unable to sleep, of lying awake during the hours of darkness as the mind and heart are without rest. As an account of restlessness and misery, the first lines are a most vivid recreation of a sleepless night. Its authenticity is stressed in the fifth line: 'With witness I speak this', which means 'as God is my witness' (God having observed the poet's lonely sleeplessness). But then the misery deepens: it was not just a night of misery, but years of it, a whole life of it: prayers and cries are unanswered by 'dearest him' (Christ), and so they are like dead letters. Then comes the fearful sestet:

> *I am gall, I am heartburn. God's most deep decree*
> *Bitter would have me taste: my taste was me;*
> *Bones built in me, flesh filled, blood brimmed the curse.*

In the middle of the night, unable to sleep, the body and the self are powerfully conscious of their own identity. Hopkins' sense of himself is of something that tastes sharp and bitter, like gall (in jaundice) or heartburn. Now the way in which an individual 'selves' takes on a dreadful aspect here: the taste of bitterness, he realizes, is himself, the inescapable self, doomed to be like this through every stage of the process – bones, flesh, blood. What is more, this seems to have been decreed by God Himself, so that there is no escape: the curse of God is confirmed at every stage, until the final result is this self that the poet loathes. This is the opposite of the joyful 'selving' of 'As kingfishers catch fire . . .': there the creatures rejoice in their own self-being, in the sounds that they make or the colours which they display. Now Hopkins feels that this is what hell is: to be punished for ever by an awareness of the loathed self, the 'sweating' self, chained for ever to the inescapable ego of greed and selfishness – only hell is even worse, unimaginable in its horror.

This poem is perhaps the most vivid of the terrible sonnets: it finds language which is able to recreate not only the experience of waking miserably in the night, but which uses images to describe frustration and anguish. The cries are like 'dead letters sent', an image for failure, pointlessness, non-communication; the self becomes like heartburn, something rising up from within as a bitter, choking sensation; the selfish yeast of the spirit sours the dull dough (as if bad yeast turned the dough sour, and made rotten bread). All these lead up to the portrait of the lost and 'their sweating selves': once again the image is a physical one, and it is extremely effective.

In addition to the imagery, the rhythm is also notable: the poem is written with swift, forward movements and sudden stops, together with short stabbing phrases. The first line, for instance, has 'not day' tacked on to the end of its main part, and the last line 'but worse'. The two appendages produce a rhythmic echo in the mind, enclosing (from lines 2 to 13) other short units and strong pauses. Consider the rhythm of

> *With witness I speak this. But where I say*
> *Hours I mean years, mean life.*

The voice in reading this (and Hopkins intended his poems to be spoken, perhaps even these ones) has to register a strong pause after 'this', and probably after the long syllable of 'Hours': 'Hours' then gives way (as if after a pause for reflection) to 'I mean years' (the hours–years echo is important in sound too) and then, after another pause for thought, 'mean life'. 'Mean life' is another of the two-word units, picking up the sound from the first line, and in every case the phrases are followed by a full stop. Longer ones are are found in 'With witness I speak this', 'I am gall, I am heartburn', and in the climactic horror of 'my taste was me'. Between these are the longer sentences, but the frequent occurrence of such short units breaks up the sonnet into fragments which are expressive of the mind itself, fragmented, exhausted, searching for the right phrase, modifying and deepening the experience into a dreadful reality. So what begins with a normal Hopkins alliteration, with words echoing and changing – 'feel . . . fell . . . dark . . . day' – becomes something very different. It is quite unlike, for example, the 'Irish' sonnet, 'To seem the stranger . . .', where the dominant pattern is for the syntactical units to work across the line endings. It is also quite unlike the sonnet which follows, 'Patience, hard thing! . . .'

'Patience, hard thing! . . .'

This sonnet is more meditative, and less beset by the horrors of mental anguish or self-loathing. It does have images of evil, such as the ivy growing round the heart, luxuriantly, 'Purple eyes and seas of liquid leaves all day', (like some awful sea-monster) or the idea that 'We hear our hearts grate on themselves' which is painful and harsh (reminiscent of 'thoughts against thoughts in groans grind' from 'Spelt from Sibyl's Leaves'). But the principal tone of the sonnet is relieved from such self-laceration by the clever analysis of patience itself, and the turning towards God at the end.

Patience is seen from two points of view: from that of the religious man, and from the point of view of the 'natural heart', the human impulses of the ordinary person. From a religious point of view found in the first five lines, patience is a hard thing to strive for, because it 'Wants war, wants wounds' (lacks war and wounds: in other words it is not one of the glamorous Christian virtues, and has none of the directness and excitement of Christian warfare). Patience is rather a wearying thing, requiring the Christian

> *To do without, take tosses, and obey.*

To understand this it is necesssary to take the third line as a parenthesis, so that the fourth line is the predicate of 'asks' (line 2):

> *... Patience who asks*
> *(Wants war, wants wounds; weary his times, his tasks;)*
> *To do without, take tosses, and obey.*

Patience, in other words, is a kind of perpetual self-denial, doing without things, accepting slights or rudeness or neglect, and obeying God. These qualities allow 'Rare patience' to root (and therefore to flourish); without them, patience can find nowhere to take root.

Our *natural* heart has its own purposes, however, and patience, once it has taken root, masks the disappointments of the natural heart, the 'ruins of wrecked past purpose'. This is obviously a good thing from the point of view of a religious; the natural heart is concealed behind this luxuriant thicket of ivy, which prevents the natural heart from brooding too much on its own selfish purposes. From a natural point of view, however, the ivy seems clinging and poisonous, and the ordinary purposes of life are now in ruins. It is as though Hopkins admires patience as a religious virtue, but is horrified by it as a destroyer of the natural self. It is this split between the religious heart and the natural heart which results in the sound of grating:

> *We hear our hearts grate on themselves: it kills*
> *To bruise them dearer.*

'Dearer' is an archaic word, meaning 'more grievously'; we can hear the sound and feel the pain of the conflict within us of the natural self and the religious self, and yet we continue, rightly, to ask God to bend our rebellious wills to His service. The alteration in word-order here –

> *... Yet the rebellious wills*
> *Of us we do bid God bend to him even so.*

– suggests even in the bending of the syntax and the odd construction across the line ('the ... wills / Of us we do bid') a certain effort, a pushing of something beyond certain limits, or out of its natural shape. But the last three lines of the sonnet emphasize not our effort but God's kindness: indeed, patience, which is so difficult for human beings, is an indication of God's goodness, since He is patient with mankind:

> *. . . He is patient. Patience fills*
> *His crisp combs, and that comes those ways we know.*

The combs are honeycombs, as if God was filling crisp honeycombs with patience for the good of mankind, like some benevolent and perennially active bee, engaged in the mysterious and magical process of making honey. So 'that comes those ways we know', that is we 'know' if we have experienced them: *we* know – the appeal is to those who have had God's delicious kindness bestowed upon them. So the poem which begins with the hardness of patience ends with its benefits to the truly religious.

'My own heart . . .'

Like the last poem, 'My own heart . . .' mixes an awareness of the severity of a truly religious life with the ultimate comfort that is to be found in the presence of God – though in this case only briefly. Here the poet's message to himself is that he ought to be more gentle with himself: it is a poem of self-compassion, and the remarkable thing about it is that it does not come out as a poem of self-pity. He seems to have earned the right to be kind to himself; but the feeling is also due to the clever use of language, the gentle simplicity of 'My own heart let me more have pity on'. It is instructive to see what the alteration of word-order has done here: in prose it would have been 'Let me have more pity on my own heart', but the poetic order complicates the meaning quite beautifully. At first it seems to the reader that Hopkins is addressing his own heart – 'My own heart, let me . . .', until it becomes clear that it is the heart which has to have pity shown to *it*; and the placing of 'more' means that the phrase 'more have pity on' is not just 'have more pity' but 'more have pity', which suggests more frequently or more abundantly.

The first four lines deal with this possibility, that the poet might be kinder and more charitable to himself, and

> *not live this tormented mind*
> *With this tormented mind tormenting yet.*

This suggests a kind of circular process, a tormented mind tormenting itself: this is because, as in the first line, the normal word-order has been reversed. If we place the first 'this tormented mind' at the end, the whole passage makes good sense but is much less effective: 'not live, with this tormented mind yet (continually, still) tormenting this tormented mind (or itself)'. The idea is circular still, but not so intricately bound together:

in Hopkins' version the whole has to be completed, like a circle, in order to make sense.

The same kind of circular movement is found in the second quatrain:

> *I cast for comfort I can no more get*
> *By groping round my comfortless, ...*

The missing word after 'comfortless' could be 'self' or 'world' (Bridges' suggestion), and the connections between 'cast' (cast about) and 'groping round', together with the echo of 'comfort ... comfortless', all carry the suggestion of going round in circles. This is followed by other images of frustration and failure: the blind man who cannot get comfort (here omitted) from the day, or the thirsty man who cannot satisfy his thirst from the sea.

The poet is reminding himself that he cannot just *decide* to be more comfortable: indeed, one of the great skills of this sonnet (and the preceding one) is the change of mood. Hopkins sets out to be more gentle, but is inexorably drawn back into the comfortless world. The sestet calls him back, calls him to order – 'Soul, self;' it is as though the soul will not listen, and has to be called again, as the self: it needs a good talking-to, and Hopkins is ordering it to pay attention.

> *Soul, self; come, poor Jackself, I do advise*
> *You, jaded, let be; call off thoughts awhile*
> *Elsewhere; leave comfort root-room;*

The speaking voice can again be heard, in a different tone, addressing the Jackself (the ordinary, common self) kindly and gently: 'I do advise' sounds like 'if you go on like this, you'll make yourself ill'. Then comes the complicated

> *let joy size*
> *At God knows when to God knows what;*

which means 'let joy grow ('size') when God wills it and to whatever extent He decides. For God disposes

> *whose smile*
> *'s not wrung, see you; unforeseen times rather – as skies*
> *Betweenpie mountains – lights a lovely mile.*

God's smiles are not forced ones, says Hopkins. Rather. at unforeseen times they lighten the traveller's way on the journey through life, just as skies 'betweenpie' the mountains. The word 'betweenpie' means to dapple between: as a magpie is 'pied', dark and light: and if a word such as 'pied' exists, then it could be the past participle of a now-forgotten verb 'to pie'. Having supposed such a verb, Hopkins combines it with 'between' so that the skies 'betweenpie' the mountains – give a brighter dappled space between the dark shapes.

The image of God's smile unexpectedly lightening the traveller's road is typical of the way in which Hopkins can register the inner moods of the mind with reference to nature. In the terrible sonnets, the pain comes in pangs and is felt in blows: relief comes as a lull in the storm, some fitful moment of respite, and sometimes, blessedly, as this kind of sunlight. The fact that Hopkins does not use anything as trite as sunshine and clouds is also characteristic: by the very detail, the particularization of the effects, he suggests the authenticity of his feelings. The result is a poetry which records, convincingly, some of the problems attendant on the life of a religious.

9. Four Late Poems

'Tom's Garland'

'Tom's Garland' is a sonnet with two additional codas, or end-pieces, each with a short line followed by two normal ones (beginning 'Undenizened' and 'In both'). It is subtitled 'upon the Unemployed'. It is not an easy poem to read, although its thick consonants and sturdy syllables require reading aloud to bring out the full effect: Hopkins is attempting to capture in verse the thick sturdiness and tough self-sufficiency of the labourer. More than most of his poems it shows the point of view of the fastidious priest, who sees the navvy as dominated by the physical needs of working, eating and sleeping:

> *he is all for his meal*
> *Sure, 's bed now.*

The abbreviation, and the placing of the words, suggests a brutish existence, concentrating on food and sleep ('he is all for . . .'). But this kind of life has its compensations: Tom doesn't fall ill, and doesn't worry:

> *seldom sick*
> *Seldomer heartsore; that treads through, prickproof, thick*
> *Thousands of thorns, thoughts . . .*

To the poet of the terrible sonnets, agonizing over his thought-thorns, there must have been something enviable about this insensitivity, just as Hopkins also seems to envy Tom's physical toughness, his ability to tread through thorns as well as thoughts. And such day-labourers, he maintains, have a part to play in the community.

Neither Bridges nor Dixon, to Hopkins' wry amusement, could understand the poem. Hopkins sent an explanation (LB 272–4, reprinted in the notes to the Penguin edition of the poems, pp. 241–2). 'Once explained,' said Hopkins triumphantly, 'how clear it all is!'

The working men, at the beginning, have steel boots, and at the end of the day Tom and his mate ('fallowbootfellow': his mate in the same kind of boots, covered with 'fallow' or unploughed earth or mud) leave their picks in a pile and make their way home, striking sparks from the road as they go with their nailed boots ('rips out rockfire homeforth'). Then come the lines describing Tom as eating and sleeping, unworried by care, unworried too about the country:

Commonweal
Little Í reck ho!

As Hopkins said – 'Here comes a violent but effective hyperbaton [inversion] or suspension,

> in which the action of the mind mimics that of the labourer – surveys his lot, low but free from care; then by a sudden strong act throws it over the shoulder or tosses it away as a light matter.

The community of which the labourer is a part is the ideal society, with the monarch as the head ('lordly head / With heaven's lights high hung round') and the labourers who dig up ('mammock') the earth ('motherground') are the mighty foot. Below the labourers, however, and cast out of the true community, are those of whom Hopkins was also very conscious – the unemployed in their misery, despair and rage. These are those who are 'nó way sped' (do not flourish) in either 'mind or mainstrength' (mind or body). They

> *gold go garlanded*
> *With, perilous, O nó; nor yet plod safe shod sound;*

They have no money ('perilous gold', perilous either because it can be stolen from them, or perhaps because it endangers the soul); they have no safe ways of walking, and maybe no proper footwear; they have no fixed abode ('Undenizened') and no hope of fame or ease in this life. Some men have money (gold) and work (steel), but these are 'bare / In both'; the only thing they do share with other people is *care*. And care is

> *by Despair, bred Hangdog dull;*

Care is (on the analogy of racehorse breeding) the sire which (by Despair) breeds the hangdog look and the dull misery on street corners; worse than this, care and rage breed not 'Hangdog' but 'Manwolf', a creature that roams in packs, destructively. Their packs 'infest the age', like a disease.

'Tom's Garland' begins in description and ends in political insight. It is an extraordinary sonnet in its compressed statement of social evil, moving from the idea of the hierarchical community to those who are outside all the benefits of community life. It is a vivid account of what is meant by unemployment, and what the consequences of unemployment are for society: and it is unusual in its ability to mix compassion and condemnation in the same lines. Hopkins was well aware of the miseries of the unemployed; he was also quick to condemn violence, rioting and destruction.

'Harry Ploughman'

'Harry Ploughman' is another poem which Hopkins said was 'altogether for recital, not for perusal' (L B 263). He even thought that it could somehow be performed, with a chorus reciting the 'burden-lines' (the short lines). This is a sonnet with twenty lines (proportioned 12 + 8) instead of the usual fourteen lines (8 + 6); but in addition to the sound and proportion of a grand sonnet, there is also a very strong pictorial element: 'I want Harry Ploughman to be a vivid picture before the mind's eye,' Hopkins told Bridges; 'if he is not that the sonnet fails.' (L B 265) Certainly the portrait of the ploughman in the first four lines is vivid, with every muscle standing out in detail – arms, 'Hard as hurdle', and 'Rope-over thigh'. Some of the description is difficult, such as the 'broth of goldish flue/Breathed round', which is usually seen as a fine fur of blond hair on the skin (broth as a kind of mixture, flue as 'a woolly or downy substance'). The other images are used to describe the shaping of a fine body – the rack of ribs, the slim waist ('scooped flank') the 'knee-nave' (knee-cap, round-shaped, like the nave of a church and surrounded by side aisles of muscle) and 'barrelled shank' (strong and muscular legs). All these sinews together make 'one crew' (line 5), and they are commanded and steered by Harry's care – 'a grey eye's heed'. Disciplined like a tight ship or a platoon of soldiers they 'fall to;/Stand at stress', every muscle ready for duty. The lines which follow ripple with movement, firm yet flexible, to suggest the way in which the muscles perform their 'sinew-service'.

In the second part of the sonnet there is a perceptible change into movement, as Harry 'leans to it'. Everything up to this point has been still, poised to move: now Harry bends and 'Back, elbow, and liquid waist/In him, all quail (give way, yield) to the wallowing o' the plough'. His cheeks redden and his hair blows in the wind. We are asked to see, too, Harry's 'Churlsgrace' (his simple country peasant's grace) and it is this grace of movement (child of his manly strength) which 'hangs or hurls' the pieces of earth; while his feet (broad feet, lashed in bluff hide – strong leather) keep pace with the furls of the ploughed earth (which race them along the furrow). The furls themselves are beautiful, turned upwards by the 'cragiron' or ploughshare beneath, cold earth yet shining, shot through with shining like a fountain.

'Harry Ploughman' is sometimes criticized as too complicated in syntax and image, and it is certainly an intricate poem: but its faults (if they are faults, and I do not believe that they are) are inextricably connected with its excellencies. Like so many of Hopkins' poems, this is a poem of acute observation; and also of admiration. Hopkins has chosen to portray a man at his work: a man whose every movement is purposeful, in harmony with the plough which he guides and follows. The action of man, plough, and earth is a complicated one: and like a painter Hopkins has portrayed it with deft word-strokes, which carry detail and broader movement. 'Wordpainting,' Hopkins told Bridges, 'is, in the verbal arts, the great success of our day;' (LB 267) in 'Harry Ploughman' Hopkins produced a masterly example of it.

'That Nature is a Heraclitean Fire and of the comfort of the Resurrection'

The Greek philosopher Heraclitus (*c.* 535–*c.* 475 BC) believed that the world was in a state of continual change, and that the ultimate reality from which all things sprang and to which all things returned was fire. By natural processes fire became air, air water, water earth, and earth returned to fire: and the world that we know and see is at some point in this ever-changing process. Hopkins loved the very fact and essence of change in nature and landscape – the seasons, the weather, the rivers and streams, the skies. One very obvious example of change is found in cloud-formations, which Hopkins loved to describe in his notebooks and poems: in this poem they are 'tossed pillows', 'heaven-roysterers'; they become sunlight or shadow on roughcast walls, or white ones, or through elm trees. Through the trees the sunlight produces 'Shivelights' (shafts of light) and 'shadowtackle' (pieces of shadow) which 'lace, lance, and pair': they make lace-patterns, dart light through trees, join together in a dance of light.

As the clouds and sunlight change, so the wind produces its own changes. It pulls like 'ropes' and wrestles, and beats out the creases of the previous day's weather (a lovely image, of the fresh wind cleaning, beating out the crumplings of the weather like someone beating out a carpet or straightening a suit). The wind is fresh and drying:

> *in pool and rut peel parches*
> *Squandering ooze to squeezed* | *dough, crust, dust;*

The wind takes the ooze in pools or on the edge of ruts ('rut peel') and parches it, squandering the water within them until they become first like squeezed-out dough, then crust, and finally dust. In the dry earth that remains there are groups of 'masks' (footmarks, like a print) and other marks of man's work, now held stiff in the dried mud ('Footfretted in it').

All these examples show the lovely changes of the natural world: behind them, Hopkins muses, is the Heraclitean fire:

> *Million-fuelèd,* | *nature's bonfire burns on.*

But the corollary of all this change is that mankind is a part of it, and his life is quickly over. Man is the 'clearest-selvèd spark' of the great fire of nature, the one with the clearest sense of himself, the most *selved* thing, yet how fast his spark of life ('firedint') and his memory in the mind of others both disappear! Everything goes into the dark night, and Hopkins laments that 'Manshape', which in every person is different ('that shone/Sheer off, disseveral, a star') is blotted out inevitably by time and death. For his solution he turns from classical Greek philosophy to the Christian hope of the Resurrection; and the section of the poem which follows depends heavily on St Paul's magnificent treatment of the subject in I Corinthians 15 –

There is one glory of the sun, and another glory of the moon, and another glory of the stars: for one star differeth from another star in glory.
So also is the resurrection of the dead . . .

For since by man came death, by man came also the resurrection of the dead.
For as in Adam all die, even so in Christ shall all be made alive.

Behold, I shew you a mystery: We shall not all sleep, but we shall all be changed,
In a moment, in the twinkling of an eye, at the last trump: for the trumpet shall sound, and the dead shall be raised incorruptible, and we shall be changed.
For this corruptible must put on incorruption, and this mortal must put on immortality. . . .

verses 41–2, 21–2, 51 3

But how wonderfully Hopkins reworks St Paul! As part of the Heraclitean process the body is left behind to the 'residuary worm' (the worm to whom it is bequeathed, like a legatee), and the Christian is suddenly changed 'at a trumpet crash' and puts on immortality – 'I am all at once what Christ is'. This is because Christ redeemed mankind ('since he was what I am'): and the most ordinary man ('Jack'), this absurd man ('joke'), this worthless man, like a piece of broken pottery ('poor potsherd'), this fool ('patch'), piece of wood ('matchwood') is *transformed*:

> *This Jack, joke, poo* | *r potsherd,* | *patch, matchwood, immortal diamond,*
>   *Is immortal diamond.*

As well as being all these foolish things, man is also an immortal diamond, for he has a soul: it is this which is preserved when the remainder is left behind. The last line and a half are marvellous in their inclusiveness, with their ideas tumbling over one another and yet controlled: they are quite unparaphrasable, and this is as it should be. Hopkins has succeeded in breathing new life into a traditional doctrine.

The poem is extremely unusual, not only in its energy, but in the distance which it travels in so short a space: as we have seen it contains both Greek philosophy and Christian doctrine, and the lengthy title itself is an indication of its extent and range of thought. At the beginning it succeeds in describing such things as clouds, and the wind drying up the puddles; but at the end it is also relating the whole principle of change to the Christian interpretation of time, death and everlasting life. Of all Hopkins' poems, it is perhaps the most inclusive: it is not, like the more famous 'The Windhover', a poem about one bird seen at a single moment, but it is a meditation on the whole of nature, and the whole of human life. It is miraculously compressed, as all of Hopkins' finest poems are: and above all, it is one of his poems which most joyously and gloriously combines the heart, the intellect and the senses.

Like 'Tom's Garland', this is a sonnet with codas, of which there are three, beginning at line 15 with a link line ('Is any of him at all so stark'), which is then followed by three triplets – two long lines and one short one. The last is notable for its skilful and unusual rhyme – ('I am, and'/'Diamond').

'Thou art indeed just, Lord . . .'

'That Nature is a Heraclitean Fire' is a poem of abundance, of joy and sadness, energy and change, culminating in the greatest transformation of all. 'Thou art indeed just . . .', on the other hand, is sadder and more reflective, and it is significant that Hopkins does not need to add codas to the sonnet on this occasion: the fourteen lines are sufficient, as they were in the terrible sonnets, to express his need. And instead of the recital effect of 'Harry Ploughman', this poem is a one-voice, slow-movement poem: it was to be read, said Hopkins, *adagio molto* (very slowly).

The quotation at the head of this sonnet is from Jeremiah 12:1:

Righteous art thou, O Lord, when I plead with thee: yet let me talk with thee of thy judgments: Wherefore doth the way of the wicked prosper? . . .

The second verse of this chapter is also worth noting: 'Thou hast planted them, yea, they have taken root: they grow, yea, they bring forth fruit. . . .' The images of rooting, growing and bringing forth fruit are taken up in the last line of Hopkins' poem, which compares the poet's sense of failure and sterility to that of a dried-up plant. It is an image which is latent throughout the previous thirteen lines: the poet feels that all his efforts are coming to nothing, and he is entering a plea of 'unfair', almost as if he were in a court of law. Twice he addresses God as 'sir', as one might address a magistrate or a chairman of the bench: yet beneath the formality and polite restraint there is a cry of anguish.

This is a subtle and affecting poem. It is not so dramatic as the terrible sonnets or 'That Nature is a Heraclitean Fire', but it has its own resonance and power. This comes principally from the conjunction in the poem of two voices. One is the restrained voice of the pleader, conducting his case according to the rules of the court; the other is the voice of a bitter and suffering individual, who feels that all he has tried to do has ended in failure and disappointment. In the poem the first voice is embodied in the formal precision of the sonnet form itself: the whole is beautifully controlled within the fourteen lines, with no codas, and with a very tight rhyme-scheme (only four rhymes: ABBA ABBA CD CD CD). Within this tight formality, however, the phrases and sentences twist and turn, and break across the lines with anxiety and emotion. The first two lines are a good example:

> *Thou art indeed just, Lord, if I contend*
> *With thee; but, sir, so what I plead is just.*

The poem opens dramatically, as if the speaker has been listening to the Lord speaking about His justice: and the word just appears in both arguments. It looks like being one of those difficult cases in which there seems to be right on both sides, so that the pleading becomes a real struggle. In this context the crucial word is 'contend': it means 'to argue a case', but also 'to struggle'. The poet is arguing his case with God, but he is also wrestling with God (as he was in the opening lines of 'The Wreck of the Deutschland'). The running over after 'contend', and the sudden stop at 'with thee' is part of a consistent pattern of breaking up the lines of this sonnet, which causes its own rhythmical tension to match the emotional stress. The 'so' in line 2 could mean 'also' or 'so too', and is probably left thus by Hopkins to allow both.

Three questions follow. The first is absolutely straightforward – 'Why do sinners' ways prosper?' followed by the inversion of 'and why must/Disappointment all I endeavour end?' The force of this unusual word placing is to force all the emphasis on to 'Disappointment' and to sharpen the contrast between '*end*eavour' and 'end'. The syllables emphasize the closeness of the two: in his trying he is always failing. The third question is even longer and more complex: it is as though the poet becomes more insistent, and the questioning becomes more pressing, more fully developed:

> *Wert thou mine enemy, O thou my friend,*
> *How wouldst thou worse, I wonder, than thou dost*
> *Defeat, thwart me?*

The rhythm and syntax are again very expressive: the two lines are one interacting series of clauses, leading gradually towards some conclusion, which turns out to be the sudden compression of 'Defeat, thwart me'.

The bitterness of the lines that follow – comparing the poet's own sense of failure with 'the sots and thralls of lust' who thrive more in their 'spare hours' than the poet in his whole life – adds pungency and salt to the plea, but it must not be overdone: so Hopkins cleverly turns the comparison away from other people to nature. Once again he is able to point to the beauty of spring, but not to celebrate it (as he did in 'Spring'): now it becomes a sad contrast. as he sees nature in all its abundance – the banks thickly leaved, the cow parsley ('fretty chervil') beside them and the whole touched by the fresh wind – and compares it to his own inability to find such growth and freshness. The birds build their nests, but the poet can do nothing. He can only 'strain' (a most expressive word, suggesting 'force' and 'make excessive demands upon himself') and not produce. 'breed', a single work that lives ('wakes'). He feels utterly sterile ('Time's eunuch') and he is like a dried-up plant that needs rain.

Although it is not as spectacular as the others, 'Thou art indeed just . . .' is one of the most affecting of Hopkins' later poems. It is a beautifully-controlled and very moving expression of the sense of failure, and it is a very good example of the way in which Hopkins' religious beliefs deepened and gave significance to his poetry. This sonnet could have been just a grumble about failure and sterility, or a bitter poem about those who seemed happier, more careless and more successful than himself. But the passage from Jeremiah, and the allusions to his own dedication and to God the righteous judge, raise the poem and give it the status of a theological problem as well as a private dilemma. The word which occurs twice in line 3 is the word 'why': it is a cry which has been made by many suffering servants from Jeremiah until now, a cry which is a question from a fallen world. And if Hopkins' later poems can be said to have anything in the way of a meaning which underpins them, it can be seen to be an acute awareness of his own and others' unhappiness. He rescues moments, attitudes, pictures, places from this (a boy

131

bugler taking communion, a man ploughing, a stream tumbling over rocks), but the note steadily deepens as Hopkins becomes more and more aware of the unhappiness of the world (or the transience of happiness) in his own experience.

Conclusion

In a letter of June 1878 to R. W. Dixon, Hopkins praised two things in Dixon's poetry:

> you have great reason to thank God who has given you so astonishingly clear an inward eye to see what is in visible nature and in the heart such a deep insight into what is earnest, tender, and pathetic in human life and feeling. (LD 9)

We may apply Hopkins' words to his own poetry without falsifying matters: there is first of all the thanks to God, from whom all human powers come; then the inward eye, which sees what is in the outer world of visible nature – the eye which tells the outer eye what to see (for a painter does not simply 'paint what he sees' but what his mind tells him to see, the dictation of his inward eye); then, thirdly, there is the heart, which, in Hopkins' view, gives an insight into that which is earnest, tender, and pathetic in human life.

As so often, Hopkins' words are carefully and exactly chosen. His own heart, in particular, is much in evidence in the poems – in its joy at the wonders of the created world, such as the windhover, and in its pain at destruction ('Binsey Poplars') or neglect. In addition to the eye and the heart, however, he might have added a mind and a hand: the fine mind that could see to the centre of a situation or a problem, and find an exact image for something, or which (as in 'That Nature is a Heraclitean Fire') could see the unifying possibilities even in such disparate elements as changing clouds, a drying wind, early Greek philosophy and Christian thought; and the craftsman's hand, which could convert his ideas into sharply-focused words and images, and could shape the rhythms in accordance with the feeling. In particular, his use of rhetorical tricks often brings out, rather than obscures, the connection that he wants to make: words take on a new significance by being put into an unexpected relationship with other words. In 'That Nature is a Heraclitean Fire' again, the a–b–b–a pattern which Hopkins was fond of (the chiasmus) is used to provide a compressed statement of the Christian belief in the redemption:

> *I am all at once what Christ is,* ¹ *since he was what I am ...*

Such craftsmanship, at its best, is part of an extraordinary precision which is the hallmark of Hopkins' poetry. It was, no doubt, connected with his character, his need to get things exactly right (part of the appeal of the Jesuits was probably that there was a certainty about it, with no half-measures). The effect is often of a piercing directness, and of an originality which produces a sense of the unexpected and extraordinary combined with the exact. This gives it an almost indescribable quality, a 'pitch' or 'temper' which is perhaps best summed up in R. W. Dixon's words, when he said that Hopkins' poems had

something that I cannot describe, but know to myself by the inadequate word *terrible pathos* something of what you call temper in poetry: a right temper which goes to the point of the terrible; the terrible crystal. (LD 80)

Suggestions for Further Reading

There are a great many books, articles and other writings about Hopkins. The following will be found generally useful:

Donald McChesney, *A Hopkins Commentary* (London, 1968)

Peter Milward, *A Commentary on G. M. Hopkins' 'The Wreck of the Deutschland'* (Tokyo, 1968)

Peter Milward, *A Commentary on the Sonnets of Gerard Manley Hopkins* (Tokyo, 1969)

Paul Mariani, *A Commentary on the Complete Poems of Gerard Manley Hopkins* (Ithaca, N.Y., 1970)

Norman H. MacKenzie, *A Reader's Guide to Gerard Manley Hopkins* (London, 1981)

The above will be found helpful in deciphering the meaning of Hopkins' poetry. General and biographical accounts include:

John Pick, *Gerard Manley Hopkins, Priest and Poet*, 2nd ed. (London, 1966)

Norman H. MacKenzie, *Gerard Manley Hopkins* (London, 1968)

Bernard Bergonzi, *Gerard Manley Hopkins* (London, 1977)

Other useful books on Hopkins include:

W. A. M. Peters, *Gerard Manley Hopkins* (London, 1948)

R. K. R. Thornton, *Gerard Manley Hopkins: The Poems* (London, 1973)

Peter Milward and Raymond V. Schoder, *Landscape and Inscape* (London, 1975)

James Milroy, *The Language of Gerard Manley Hopkins* (London, 1977)

There is also a discriminating 'Casebook' (documents, critical essays):

Margaret Bottrall (ed.), *Gerard Manley Hopkins, Poems* (London, 1975)

Index of Poems and Subjects

Subjects

READ MORE IN PENGUIN

In every corner of the world, on every subject under the sun, Penguin represents quality and variety – the very best in publishing today.

For complete information about books available from Penguin – including Puffins, Penguin Classics and Arkana – and how to order them, write to us at the appropriate address below. Please note that for copyright reasons the selection of books varies from country to country.

In the United Kingdom: Please write to *Dept. JC, Penguin Books Ltd, FREEPOST, West Drayton, Middlesex UB7 OBR*

If you have any difficulty in obtaining a title, please send your order with the correct money, plus ten per cent for postage and packaging, to *PO Box No. 11, West Drayton, Middlesex UB7 OBR*

In the United States: Please write to *Penguin USA Inc., 375 Hudson Street, New York, NY 10014*

In Canada: Please write to *Penguin Books Canada Ltd, 10 Alcorn Avenue, Suite 300, Toronto, Ontario M4V 3B2*

In Australia: Please write to *Penguin Books Australia Ltd, 487 Maroondah Highway, Ringwood, Victoria 3134*

In New Zealand: Please write to *Penguin Books (NZ) Ltd, 182–190 Wairau Road, Private Bag, Takapuna, Auckland 9*

In India: Please write to *Penguin Books India Pvt Ltd, 706 Eros Apartments, 56 Nehru Place, New Delhi 110 019*

In the Netherlands: Please write to *Penguin Books Netherlands B.V., Keizersgracht 231 NL–1016 DV Amsterdam*

In Germany: Please write to *Penguin Books Deutschland GmbH, Friedrichstrasse 10–12, W–6000 Frankfurt/Main 1*

In Spain: Please write to *Penguin Books S. A., C. San Bernardo 117–6° E–28015 Madrid*

In Italy: Please write to *Penguin Italia s.r.l., Via Felice Casati 20, I–20124 Milano*

In France: Please write to *Penguin France S. A., 17 rue Lejeune, F–31000 Toulouse*

In Japan: Please write to *Penguin Books Japan, Ishikiribashi Building, 2–5–4, Suido, Tokyo 112*

In Greece: Please write to *Penguin Hellas Ltd, Dimocritou 3, GR–106 71 Athens*

In South Africa: Please write to *Longman Penguin Southern Africa (Pty) Ltd, Private Bag X08, Bertsham 2013*

READ MORE IN PENGUIN

PLAYS IN PENGUIN

Edward Albee   Who's Afraid of Virginia Woolf?

Alan Ayckbourn   The Norman Conquests

Bertolt Brecht   Parables for the Theatre (The Good Woman of Setzuan/The
    Caucasian Chalk Circle)

Anton Chekhov   Plays (The Cherry Orchard/Three Sisters/Ivanov/The
    Seagull/Uncle Vanya)

Henrik Ibsen   Hedda Gabler/The Pillars of the Community/The Wild Duck

Eugène Ionesco   Absurd Drama (Rhinoceros/The Chair/The Lesson)

Ben Jonson   Three Comedies (Volpone/The Alchemist/Bartholomew Fair)

D. H. Lawrence   Three Plays (The Collier's Friday Night/
    The Daughter-in-Law/The Widowing of Mrs Holroyd)

Arthur Miller   Death of a Salesman

John Mortimer   A Voyage Round My Father/What Shall We Tell Caroline?/
    The Dock Brief

J. B. Priestley   Time and the Conways/I Have Been Here Before/An
    Inspector Calls/The Linden Tree

Peter Shaffer   Lettice and Lovage/Yonadab

Bernard Shaw   Plays Pleasant (Arms and the Man/Candida/The Man of
    Destiny/You Never Can Tell)

Sophocles   Three Theban Plays (Oedipus the King/Antigone/Oedipus at
    Colonus)

Arnold Wesker   Plays, Volume 1: The Wesker Trilogy (Chicken Soup with
    Barley/Roots/I'm Talking about Jerusalem)

Oscar Wilde   Plays (Lady Windermere's Fan/A Woman of No Importance/
    An Ideal Husband/The Importance of Being Earnest/Salome)

Thornton Wilder   Our Town/The Skin of Our Teeth/The Matchmaker

Tennessee Williams   Sweet Bird of Youth/A Streetcar Named Desire/The
    Glass Menagerie

READ MORE IN PENGUIN

PENGUIN BOOKS OF POETRY

American Verse
British Poetry Since 1945
Caribbean Verse in English
A Choice of Comic and Curious Verse
Contemporary American Poetry
Contemporary British Poetry
English Christian Verse
English Poetry 1918–60
English Romantic Verse
English Verse
First World War Poetry
Greek Verse
Irish Verse
Light Verse
Love Poetry
The Metaphysical Poets
Modern African Poetry
New Poetry
Poetry of the Thirties
Post-War Russian Poetry
Scottish Verse
Southern African Verse
Spanish Civil War Verse
Spanish Verse
Women Poets

READ MORE IN PENGUIN

PENGUIN POETRY LIBRARY

Arnold   Selected by Kenneth Allott
Blake   Selected by W. H. Stevenson
Browning   Selected by Daniel Karlin
Burns   Selected by W. Beattie and H. W. Meikle
Byron   Selected by A. S. B. Glover
Coleridge   Selected by Kathleen Raine
Donne   Selected by John Hayward
Dryden   Selected by Douglas Grant
Hardy   Selected by David Wright
Herbert   Selected by W. H. Auden
Keats   Selected by John Barnard
Kipling   Selected by James Cochrane
Lawrence   Selected by Keith Sagar
Milton   Selected by Laurence D. Lerner
Pope   Selected by Douglas Grant
Shelley   Selected by Isabel Quigley
Tennyson   Selected by W. E. Williams
Wordsworth   Selected by W. E. Williams

READ MORE IN PENGUIN

LITERARY BIOGRAPHIES AND AUTOBIOGRAPHIES

Sylvia Beach and the Lost Generation   Noel Riley Fitch
Joseph Conrad   Jocelyn Baines
The Making of Charles Dickens   Christopher Hibbert
A Sort of Life   Graham Greene
The Young Thomas Hardy   Robert Gittings
Ernest Hemingway   Carlos Baker
John Keats   Robert Gittings
Rudyard Kipling   Charles Carrington
How I Grew   Mary McCarthy
Katherine Mansfield: A Secret Life   Claire Tomalin
Prick Up Your Ears: The Biography of Joe Orton   John Lahr
A Better Class of Person   John Osborne
Ezra Pound   Noel Stock
Sartre: Romantic Rationalist   Iris Murdoch
Shelley   Richard Holmes
The Autobiography of Alice B. Toklas   Gertrude Stein
Lytton Strachey   Michael Holroyd
Dylan Thomas   Paul Ferris
Tolstoy   Henry Troyat
Tolstoy   A. N. Wilson
Anthony Trollope   James Pope-Hennessy
The Diaries of Evelyn Waugh
Walt Whitman   Paul Zweig
Oscar Wilde   Hesketh Pearson
Oscar Wilde   Richard Ellmann
Yeats: The Man and the Mask   Richard Ellmann

READ MORE IN PENGUIN

PENGUIN CRITICAL STUDIES

Described by *The Times Educational Supplement* as 'admirable' and 'superb', Penguin Critical Studies is a specially developed series of critical essays on the major works of literature for use by students in universities, colleges and schools.

titles published or in preparation include:

Absalom and Achitophel
The Alchemist
William Blake
The Changeling
Doctor Faustus
Dombey and Son
Don Juan and Other Poems
Emma *and* Persuasion
Great Expectations
The Great Gatsby
Gulliver's Travels
Heart of Darkness
The Poetry of Gerard
   Manley Hopkins
Jane Eyre
Joseph Andrews
Mansfield Park
Middlemarch
The Mill on the Floss
Milton's Shorter Poems
Nostromo

Paradise Lost
A Passage to India
The Poetry of Alexander Pope
Portrait of a Lady
A Portrait of the Artist as a
   Young Man
Return of the Native
Rosenkrantz and Guildenstern
   are Dead
Sons and Lovers
Tennyson
The Waste Land
Tess of the D'Urbervilles
The White Devil/
   The Duchess of Malfi
Wordsworth
Wuthering Heights
Yeats